brilliant

idea

D1099292

Prentice Hall LIFE

If life is what you make it, then making it better starts here.

What we learn today can change our lives tomorrow. It can change our goals or change our minds; open up new opportunities or simply inspire us to make a difference. That's why we have created a new breed of books that do more to help you make more of *your* life.

Whether you want more confidence or less stress, a new skill or a different perspective, we've designed *Prentice Hall Life* books to help you to make a change for the better. Together with our authors we share a commitment to bring you the brightest ideas and best ways to manage your life, work and wealth.

In these pages we hope you'll find the ideas you need for the life *you* want. Go on, help yourself.

It's what you make it

* * *

idea

Douglas Miller

PEARSON

Prentice Hall

Pearson Education Limited
Edinburgh Gate
Harlow
Essex CM20 2JE
England

© Douglas Miller 2007

First published 2007

ISBN 978-0-273-71480-4

Commissioning editor: Emma Shackleton
Project editor: Patricia Burgess
Text editor: Sarah Sutton
Designer: Kevin O'Connor
Cover designer: R&D&Co Ltd
Illustrator: Chris Long
Production controller: Franco Forgione

Printed and bound by Henry Ling, UK

The Publisher's policy is to use paper manufactured from sustainable forests.

Contents

Introduction

The idea is all there is.   Ornette Coleman, musician

You are brilliant! Sometimes it might not feel that way, but you are. As you look around the office or the train or a café or wherever you are reading this, it may be hard to believe that your fellow inhabitants on Earth share this talent with you. Just like you, they too are brilliant.

You are brilliant because you have ideas all the time. You have eureka moments when ideas jump into your head from what seems like nowhere, often at inconvenient times, like 3 a.m. Or when you are taking a shower or walking in the park or when staring out of a window for hours on end.

You are brilliant because even when undertaking the simplest or most instinctive tasks, you are capable of asking yourself questions such as 'Why don't I do it that way?' or 'I wonder what would happen if I did it this way'. You have an endless capacity to innovate.

You are brilliant because you have insights that are unique to you, that can change your own life and the lives of others too for the better.

You are brilliant because you can liberate yourself from rigid ways of thinking. You can change the way you think and change the way you approach your existing job.

You are brilliant because you can shape your world in the way you want to. Our fellow animals have to adapt themselves to their environment. You can do this too, but you can also shape your environment to suit you. You can endlessly explore and experiment with the ideas and options available to you.

So, do you want to have more brilliant ideas? Do you want to make the most of this brilliance? And do you want to know why you should? Then read on...

Why have brilliant ideas?

- At the end of your working life do you want to be able to say to yourself that you had a go? Or do you want to let all the opportunities associated with your daytime occupation slip through your hands?

- Work can be 45 years of drudgery, or the very thing that defines your life in the most positive of ways. It is not luck that separates the engaged from the psychologically retired. It is attitude.

- You are going to spend between 80,000 and 100,000 hours of your life at work. That's an awfully long time to be bored, disengaged and unstimulated. Having ideas and trying them out creates a real engagement with your work.

- You have great ideas at work all the time. What a fantastic thing to be able to say that you had a great idea, you acted on it and you made a difference.

- When we start to 'play' with our ideas we forget that we are at 'work'. We feel 'beyond time', unstressed and productive. The usual eight hours (or maybe 10 or 12) fly by. 'Work' and all the negative connotations on that word become something that other people do.

- We all like to be associated with success. Why not be part of that success by voicing your own ideas? Why not be a player rather than a watcher?

- Having ideas, trying them out and not being afraid to fail sometimes are crucial to what makes you a human being.

- Turning ideas into action is a great way to achieve a sense of personal empowerment and success. You get that feeling of 'being alive' that only true engagement with the world can bring you.

To survive and thrive your organisation needs you to show initiative, have ideas and participate.

Why are you reading this book?

Do you have an idea that is 'brilliantly simple' – a simple thing that changes something? Or are you hungry to create something 'simply brilliant' – a big thing that changes everything?

Do you have a good commercial idea or an idea for organisational change and want to know how to influence others to make things happen?

Perhaps you want more from your job – or you want to do what you do more efficiently.

You may be getting paid to be an ideas generator and feel you have run out of good ideas. You may work in an administrative role and want to bring about change or start seeing your job differently.

Perhaps you are just curious to know how to have brilliant ideas.

Whatever your role – whether a manager who wants your team to generate and implement brilliant ideas, a manager who wants to generate and implement brilliant ideas yourself, or an employee who wants to make a difference – this book is for you.

If you are all or any of those things, this is a book that can help you.

Where can you use it?

The advice in this book is geared towards those who are employed by somebody else, but many of the tools, techniques and processes are applicable in many walks of life. It is for those who feel that with the right idea they could change the world, as well as for all those who want to transform their job.

How does this book work?

Brilliant Idea takes you through the following stages:

Stage 1: Identify your goal will enable you to identify problem-solving or opportunity-taking goals that create the need for brilliant ideas.

Stage 2: Generate brilliant ideas will help you to generate brilliant ideas to achieve those goals.

Stage 3: Decision-making explains ways to select the best of those brilliant ideas.

Stage 4: Ideas in the wild shows you how to put your brilliant ideas into action through your own positive attitude and through great strategy, as well as through and with other people.

Stage 5: What happens next explains that idea generation is not a once-in-a-lifetime occurrence; it is an ongoing process. This stage helps you to see where you are in the idea cycle and where to go next.

We begin with Stage 1 – identifying problems or opportunities and setting our goals...

The brilliant idea goal

CHAPTER 1

Why have ideas?

The need to generate brilliant ideas will come from one of three sources:

1 You have identified an opportunity that needs to be brought to life. Your goal is to generate brilliant ideas that will optimise that opportunity.

2 You, your team, your department or your organisation has a problem that needs solving. Your goal is to generate brilliant ideas that will solve the problem.

3 You have had a brilliant idea and know it has potential. Your goal is to assess its potential and to decide who needs it, how it can be used, and how to get it accepted. Will it be used to solve a problem, or does it represent an opportunity to be taken?

In this chapter we look at the value of ideas and the need to transform them into goals if they are to be brought to life. We also consider how we can identify those goals. Goals give us direction, and if we know where we are heading, our thinking (our 'idea generation') becomes sharper. We look at this process in detail in Stages 2, 3 and 4.

> *A clear goal provides focus and energy and control for the idea.*
>
> James Adams
> *Conceptual Blockbusting*

As many have pointed out before, there is often little difference between a problem and an opportunity. Problems often create opportunities, and opportunities often generate problems along the way. However, the process of generating ideas remains the same, whatever our eventual goal.

The 'flow' of brilliant ideas

You can see from the flow diagram below how the identification of the goal fits into the whole brilliant idea process.

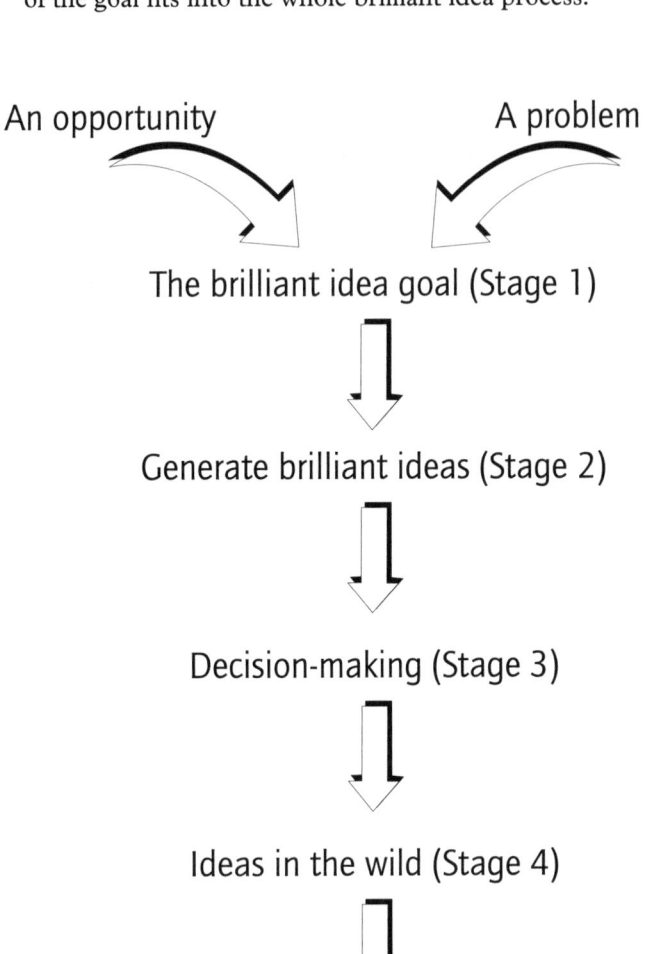

The opportunity-taking goal

An exciting route to generating a brilliant idea goal is to spot an opportunity or just have a vague notion that something might be a 'good idea'. Ideas arise when you spot an opportunity for change or gain. There is no single widely used method for spotting opportunities. What we do know is that opportunity spotters have high levels of curiosity: they ask questions and they explore. In addition, they often show dissatisfaction with the status quo because they ask lots of 'how'-type questions, with words such as *improve, better, faster, longer or quicker* attached, to improve current practices or invent new ones.

This opportunity-taking section is divided into four parts:

1 Opportunity spotters – the traits

2 'Imagineering' new ideas – creative opportunity spotting

3 Scenario thinking – a strategic approach to opportunity spotting

4 Opportunities – some reminders

Opportunity spotters – the traits

There are several characteristics that set opportunity spotters apart, and we explore them below and overleaf.

No problem

Opportunity spotters explore ideas, even though there may be no clear compelling reason to do so. Early proactive thinking can short-circuit the possibility of future problems. This is because opportunity spotters may be so early in identifying future opportunities for change that they start generating new ideas before potential problems show up in the current situation. Of course, proof of this is tough to find because if an opportunity is taken early, we are never likely to know what the consequences of not acting might have been. What we do know is that a good idea that opens up a new opportunity gives us the chance to act first before someone else does.

Possibilities

The opportunity spotter regards new ideas as possibilities and opportunities that are fun to think about. Indeed, most of us, bar the most mentally lethargic, have new ideas and create possibilities in our mind all the time. Good opportunity spotters ask questions such as, 'Why don't we do this?', or voice thoughts such as 'I wonder what would happen if...' or 'I can't believe they haven't thought of that'. Good opportunity spotters have ideas and suggest possibilities to themselves.

However, failure to act on these thoughts may trigger later regret or jealousy statements, such as 'I thought of that too' or 'They got lucky', when someone else has the same idea and acts first.

Other people's ideas

Opportunity spotters may adapt or use the ideas of others. They are good listeners, and it often requires the asking of good questions to get the valuable answers to listen to. Opportunity spotters sharpen their peripheral vision so that they see what others are saying and doing. Be alive to the opportunities and ideas that others present to you.

Creativity

Spotting opportunities often requires a high degree of creative thinking. You will find Chapter 4, 'How to Generate Brilliant Ideas', useful here.

Spotter or taker?

Opportunity spotting is one thing; opportunity taking is quite another. Once you have spotted an opportunity, you need to identify the opportunity-taking goal – what it is that you are actually trying to achieve. You need to do this because vague ideas about opportunities will generate vague solutions and vague actions. The initial opportunity will fail through lack of specificity.

Read the thought process behind 'The problem-solving goal' (see page 16) to help you define your opportunity-taking goal too.

Imagineering new ideas

Two people may have a similar idea, but they will never envisage exactly the same thing at the same time, or in exactly the same way. A new idea is always generated by one person, even if it was influenced by many. That idea may immediately be adopted by others, bent, improved, distorted or otherwise changed, but it came from one person. Why shouldn't that person be you?

A great way to spot opportunities is to 'imagineer' them – to engineer creatively through imagination. Imagineering is used in two worlds – the worlds of science and cinematography. Both these groups recognise that the ideas for new inventions – say, the aeroplane or the bicycle; Donald Duck or ET – come not from hard, reasoned thinking or statistical analysis, but from leaps in imagination with a healthy dose of intuition to back the invention.

 **brilliant** Great ideas from imagineers

For nearly 60 years the Walt Disney Corporation has had an imagineering department that dreams up new experiences for children and adults that get filtered into theme parks, characters and so forth.

What made the Apple team create the iMac and the iPod? What made the Google team create Google Earth? What made Walt Disney think of the feature-film length film *Snow White and the Seven Dwarfs* when animated movies had traditionally lasted about five minutes? What made a software developer decide that a weighty document could be sent from one country to another and arrive 10 seconds later? These things happened because in each case one person's imagination created the opportunity, intuition then told that person and others that it was a brilliant idea, and their combined creative energy made the possibility a reality.

In imagineering there is no blueprint to follow. The inspiration for ideas comes first, from a combination of imagination and intuition, and then lots of perspiration makes the fruits of your imagination come true. As the films of Walt Disney remind me and my young daughters every time we watch them, 'Dreams can come true'. That statement, as saccharine as it may be, reminds me that nothing great happens to those who do not imagine great things.

Scenario thinking – a strategic approach to opportunity spotting

Popularised by Shell in the early 1970s, scenario thinking was used as a means to predict different possible scenarios for the future of the oil industry. Shell hoped it would make them better prepared if any of those envisaged futures become real. Scenario planning is a great catalyst for creating opportunities because it takes your thinking into the future and encourages you :

Either to bring that imagined future closer or right up to now – what we might call 'future now'.

Or to identify future problems and create mechanisms that avert them or turn them into opportunities, as Shell did so successfully.

In Shell's case, this meant that when the price of oil catapulted, the company was able to grab the market share because it had mentally prepared the scenario in advance.

The thinking caught on, and organisations such as the South African mining giant Anglo-American created their own scenario-thinking department led by futurologist and scenario planner Clem Sunter. It successfully planned the scenario for the breakdown of the apartheid system.

You might decide that 'future now' is too soon for you to act, but by doing all your thinking and planning in advance, you will have a head start over those who don't.

> *What we call luck ... is what happens when preparation meets opportunity. If you stay ready, you ain't gotta get ready.*
>
> Will Smith,
> actor

Opportunities – some reminders

Here are some key things to remember in your quest to spot and then make the most of your opportunities. Many of them inject a healthy and necessary sense of realism into your thinking.

- Sometimes opportunities exist for only a short time. Be ready to put your idea into action fast.

- Look for, rather than wait for, opportunities. Those who wait see less than those who look. Waiting means you get to see only what passes directly in front of you.

- Ideas often evolve from knowledge and learning. The more informed we are, the more we can 'see'.

- On the other hand, ideas often come from naivety. That naivety can prevent us being overly bound to the old way. Naivety can liberate our thinking.

- Ideas bring uncertainty. Taking opportunities means taking risks. Nothing is guaranteed.

- Ideas and opportunities can bring problems too.

- When you take an opportunity and action an idea, things often change forever.

- Opportunities can be imagined and then forgotten, so make a note of the random ideas that jump into your head.

- New ideas often hit us when we least expect them, and, as a result, we may not be prepared for them.

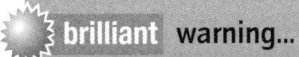 **warning...**

Not acting on our ideas when an opportunity arises might actually create problems in the long term. Why not act now and be an opportunity taker rather than wait too long and become a problem solver?*

* Readers who want to know more about spotting and taking opportunities might like to refer to my book *Make Your Own Good Fortune: How to Seize Life's Opportunities* (see page 180).

The problem-solving goal

A second route to the creation of a brilliant idea goal is to create a goal that solves a problem. As is common knowledge, the solution to a problem may well be an opportunity in itself, and, indeed, the formulation of a problem-solving goal must be an opportunity too – an opportunity to solve a problem.

The definition of the problem-solving goal (for which we will need to generate our brilliant ideas) comes in three stages:

1 Is there a problem?
2 What exactly is the problem?
3 What is the reason for the problem?

1. Is there a problem?

If you feel that your organisation has a problem, on what basis might you be saying so? Your opinion is likely to be based on one of two things:

Evidence – a specific incident or event that has highlighted a problem. You may have statistical evidence that there is a problem. If that is the case, then you move on to the next step – defining exactly what the problem is.

OR

Gut feeling – a sense that something isn't right. This may be particularly true in relation to human behaviour, where measures are difficult (and some might say undesirable). You may have an expectation of a particular standard and 'feel' that the standard isn't being met. Perhaps something isn't happening that should be happening.

It may well be that the gut feeling comes first and that you are then able to generate some evidence to support this feeling.

This stage of the whole brilliant idea process should not be underestimated. The gathering of evidence creates a much more powerful story to 'sell' to the reluctant when it comes to surmounting potential resistance to your idea (see chapters 5 and 9). It can be harder to sell your solution to a particular problem if you do not have enough evidence to convince your colleagues that there is a problem to overcome. 'I just feel it...' is not compelling on its own. The need to sell your idea starts here and now.

Having decided that there is a problem, we then move on to defining precisely what it is.

2. What exactly is the problem?

Having decided that there is a problem, the next step is to define what the problem is.

Let's say that a company decided that its people weren't communicating enough. They had some evidence for this, so they all sat down and thought up lots of ways they could communicate better. These included: reduce paper, talk more, have more meetings, cut email, have more team evenings out, increase awaydays, and make courses in communication skills compulsory.

These were all useful suggestions, but they helped only marginally; indeed, some were very vague and difficult to action. Someone then suggested that the real problem wasn't about communicating per se. The real problem seemed to be that nobody talked things through any more. Someone else pointed out that he received an average of 50 emails a day, and to him this was the root cause of the communication problem. Perhaps, he suggested, people were using email to communicate when talking would be better. Everyone seemed to agree – email was the problem; in particular the overuse of email. At this stage they were still relying on a strong element of gut feeling backed up by some evidence, namely, someone saying that he received around 50 emails a day.

Sometimes statistics will allow you to focus directly on what the problem is. In other cases a clear focus on the key questions of what, why and when the problem occurs will sharpen your thinking. A focus on what the problem is not is also important. In our example the problem was not lack of communication. It was the inappropriate use of communication methods – email in particular.

The lessons to be learnt from this scenario are therefore:

- The definition of a problem is often more important than the solutions generated because if the solutions don't actually solve the real problem, they are peripheral to our needs.

- If you are generating brilliant ideas to solve a problem, make sure you are solving the right problem.

- Be absolutely specific what the problem is.

- Make sure you focus only on solving problems that are worth your time and consideration.

3. What is the reason for the problem?

Sometimes the cause of a problem is less than clear cut. There may be more than one cause, so a 'bigger brush' solution might be needed. In our example there may be a number of causes (and a wide range of ideas to solve the problem):

- Too much cc-ing of email 'because you might be interested'.

- Too much 'management by email'.

- People sending emails to those sitting next to them.

> Concentrate on the true cause of a problem as this will generate a more focused solution.

However, it is important to try to concentrate on the true cause of a problem because it will allow the range of ideas you generate in the next stage to be more directly focused. Our company came up with the following problem-solving goal:

To reduce the amount of email so that we talk to each other more.

They decided that the best way to achieve this goal would be to come up with some problem-solving ideas. These included:

- Ban sending emails to anyone who sits within 5 metres of you.
- Make Friday an email-free day.
- Introduce a cc maximum of six people.
- Use email only as written confirmation of verbal agreements.

Then, in order to get people to talk more, they came up with a revised goal:

To reduce the level of inter-company email so that no one sends more than 15 per day.

This, arguably, is better in that it includes a standard (15 per day) that can be measured over time. Setting a standard enables you to see whether the ideas generated to solve the problem are working. The revised goal allowed them to come up with some extra problem-solving ideas:

- Set up auto-response to email so that external recipients know the mail has been received and read.
- Telephone colleagues or speak to them face to face (but keep it brief and focused).
- Everyone has to talk to a minimum of 10 people per working day.
- Recipients of emails are allowed to send replies asking, 'Why did you send me this email?' if they deem it unnecessary.
- The abbreviation 'FYI' is banned in emails.

Summary

Your idea will either solve a problem or suggest an opportunity to be taken – or both. Your idea will now become transformed into a goal. Where possible, the goal should have three characteristics:

1   It should be specific.

2   It should be energising, as you have to be motivated to achieve it.

3   It should, where appropriate, include some sort of measurement so that you can gauge progress.

We can now move forward into Stage 2 of the brilliant idea process, where we take the goal and generate lots of ideas to maximise the possibility that the goal offers us.

Generate
brilliant ideas

CHAPTER 2

'Habitats' for brilliant ideas

Our personality traits influence the ways in which we have our best ideas. Some of us have them at random: ideas pop into our head at strange times, often when we are at our most relaxed and spontaneous. Others may prefer a more systematic process for generating different kinds of ideas – perhaps a system that helps them to understand why they are thinking the way they are thinking.

Loosening the mind

However we go about generating ideas, we all have blocks that stop us short of generating all the great ideas of which we are capable. Germinating and generating ideas mean loosening the mind and the imagination. To do this we need to create the best creative conditions.

In the following two chapters we look at 'mind-loosening' in two ways. They are:

1 Creating mental 'habitats' – the environmental conditions that lead the mind into healthy idea-generation mode.

2 Releasing emotional and mental blocks – perceptions that inhibit our ability to think freely and generate brilliant ideas.

Six mental 'habitats' for brilliant ideas

In this chapter we look at six psychological or physical environments that help create the right conditions to loosen up for brilliant idea generation. The habitats are:

1 The slow lane
2 The fridge
3 The jungle
4 The playground
5 The countryside
6 The mountain

Habitat 1 – the slow lane

The old saying goes: 'Slow down or nothing worthwhile will ever catch up with you'. Sometimes we force ourselves to produce ideas and solutions under pressure, which makes it far less likely that we will come up with our best ones.

When you take yourself away from the problem or opportunity goal your 'nether mind', the one that works on a deeper level – subconscious, asleep and unconscious – is still playing with what your conscious mind has let go. The brain makes all kinds of random connections, even though you will not be conscious of it doing so. And often you find solutions, ideas and innovations jumping into your mind from your imagination because you have given your brain time to really get to work. It is not for nothing that 'let me sleep on it' works for so many of us in both decision-making and brilliant-idea generation.

Why choose the slow lane?

- If we really want to have a 'harvest' of ideas, we need to give the seeds that produce the crop time to grow and mature.

- Great 'eureka' moments don't generally occur at times of crisis. A calm mind is often a mind capable of insightful inspiration.

- It is less important to understand how your nether mind works than it is to give it time to work.

I sit and wait. It takes a lot of silence before the right line will come. I have to wait until something comes that I don't expect, something that surprises me but that I know is right.

Scott Walker,
singer and songwriter

Habitat 2 – the fridge

The fridge is about keeping yourself in check – when your emotions threaten to hijack your reason. It is about learning to keep your cool in any situation, pressurised or not.

Have you ever noticed how different people react in tough situations? How some people create a crisis out of a minor challenge? For example, the people who walk around the office with clenched fists and frowns on their faces saying, 'We've got to solve this problem now', are often the people least likely to come up with solutions. They create lots of heat, but most of us aren't at our best in the heat. It can be toughest to come up with brilliant ideas when you are trying to think 'hard' rather than think 'soft' for solutions.

Why choose the fridge?

- Tension and stress reduce the supply of oxygen to the brain, and oxygen is essential if the brain is going to work at its freest and best, without overheating.

- Keeping cool maintains perspective, helping you to understand what is a real crisis demanding an immediate response and where you have some time to play with.

- Keeping cool, even in the heat of a challenging situation, keeps the brain freshest and more able to generate a wealth of brilliant ideas.

- Keeping cool allows time for the best ideas to come to you rather than having to force yourself to find them.

- Keeping cool, especially during crises, allows you to select the best solution, even if the options are limited.

Habitat 3 – the jungle

Every species of living thing has evolved through survival in its natural habitat. That habitat includes predators (your competitors?) and all the best things that nature has to offer for your healthy survival.

Have you noticed that farmed salmon doesn't taste as good as the wild version, or that a free-range chicken has a better flavour than a battery 'broiler'? Or the way a tomato grown outdoors in the sun is sweeter than one grown in a greenhouse?

What keeps the Apple Corporation so innovative? Microsoft does – and Apple keeps Microsoft on its toes too. The competition between Starbucks and many other chains of coffee bars encourages them to keep their service levels, product innovation and business model tight, while the running of the business itself remains loose and flexible. Where else would someone have been spurred to come up with the pumpkin spice frappuccino?

Why choose the jungle?

- Welcome competition – it brings out the best in you and keeps you responsive to the market.

- Enjoy being number two or three or four in the market-place. The scent of prey out there keeps you sharp.

- Being in the jungle accelerates the need for you to create your own competition, as well as to challenge your competitors. Your next great product or service idea may well make your last one obsolete, and it's much better if you, rather than someone else, discover this.

Habitat 4 – the playground

When you experience at work the feelings of enjoyment you normally get from doing something outside the work context, work can be described as 'play'. Imagine yourself right now doing some of the activities or hobbies you like doing outside work. How do you feel? Engrossed, engaged, no sense of time, challenged, interested, turned on, tuned in, unstressed, willing to learn more and happy to make mistakes in the act of trying something? Imagine what could happen if we had those feelings at work on a more regular basis. Imagine what we might be capable of. Imagine the ideas we might have and the consequent energy we would feel for putting those ideas into action.

Being able to play at work means not feeling trapped. It means not being depressed. It means taking the uniqueness of you and using it for your benefit and the organisation you work for. It's really OK to see the workplace as a bit like a playground – to bring some of the open thinking you use so well outside work into the workplace. The playground is a positive attitude of mind. It's not about mucking around: it's about you being you.

The way you 'play' is unique to you. Nobody can tell you what form your play will take, but this is what it will *feel* like:

● Playing is simply the mindset you have when you are enjoying what you are doing.

● Playing means being yourself.

● Play creates positive pressure, but not negative stress.

● Play means you don't spend your time looking at the clock.

● Play means taking your work seriously and yourself lightly.

● Play is non-laborious activity.

● Play can mean being able to separate your behaviour from specific motives. Having specific motives gets you to the moon. Unconditional play gets you to the stars.

● Play can mean the generation of new habits, practices, products and services from stimulating workplace interactions.

Why choose the playground?

● Play allows you to generate ideas, solve problems and explore with an open mind.

A playful mind is one that embraces influences with an open mind – this wider mental panorama leads to an increased number of ideas and possible solutions.

● Play allows a wider range of possibilities than would be the case in a traditional working environment.

Because 'play' has not traditionally been associated with work, organisations traditionally haven't had the benefit of all the ideas that a playful approach brings.

● Play is productive.

It is productive because it is stimulating.

● Play challenges dull routine.

Routine does not create the environment in which we can be experimental and innovative with our ideas. Play does.

● Play allows you to use your imagination.

The use of our imagination is essential to idea generation.

● Play is what allows your organisation to change direction when it needs to because play allows for the possibility that other ways exist.

Fans of TINA (There Is No Alternative) are not noted for their playful, open-minded side.

● Play is a social lubricant, allowing us to build stronger workplace relationships.

We spark off each other when at play, which allows us to have great ideas and also to 'piggyback' each other's ideas.

Play – the business case

Success in the 21st century will come from innovation, fresh thinking and keeping ahead of the others. Individuals and organisations at play will 'tickle the customer' in a way that the non-players (your competitors) cannot hope to. To achieve this we have to start thinking in ways that we know competitors are not. So much of what passes for innovation in organisations means merely copying others. When we are at work we imitate because we can't engage enough to innovate. This might be effective in the short term, but it doesn't address the need for breakthrough thinking in the medium and long term. Play allows for innovation rather than imitation.

> Innovate rather than imitate to keep ahead of the competition and make long-term gains.

The future for all organisations is unknown. We spend fortunes on trying to predict that future, but can never truly do so. Play allows us to embrace that unknown and be entertained by the possibilities we can generate to help fill that unknown void. Rather than predict the future, play allows us to create it.

Before you are wise. After you are wise. In between you are otherwise. And in the middle is Life.

Osho Rajneesh,
spiritual teacher

Habitat 5 – the countryside

Living constantly with a problem or opportunity can make you less able to come up with the great breakthrough. The need for the 'big idea' becomes all-pervasive and the brain gets cluttered because we are thinking about little else. It is time to get away. Time to freshen up. Time to oxygenate the creative imagination.

Getting away is less about having a long weekend break (although that helps) and more about the way it will make you feel at the end of it. If you live in a town or city, go away for a day or two. Get out to the country or to an environment with a different ambience.

Try setting yourself a 'sensory pentathlon'. This means seeking experiences that will actively stimulate the five senses of taste, touch, smell, hearing and sight in different ways. Sensory pleasure is stimulating and reinvigorating, whereas a continuous and relentless focus on problems and challenges may well stifle stimulation. Ask yourself the question, 'When was the last time I did something for the first time?' as a further stimulus to restful, reinvigorating action.

Why choose the countryside?

- Only by removing yourself totally from a problem or opportunity for a time do you completely cleanse your thinking of the detritus you have picked up along the way.

- Brilliant ideas come from a variety of stimuli. Sometimes you need to tickle your imagination by putting yourself into new surroundings to avail yourself of all the creative stimuli available to you.

- Human beings are intelligent, so we can easily get bored. Boredom often leads to mental sterility. Change, even temporary change, will challenge that sterility.

- A rest relaxes your approach towards the problem or opportunity. It cleanses your mind. You start afresh.

Habitat 6 – the mountain

Gipsy Hill is one of London's steepest slopes and a challenge to the amateur cyclist. It is also one of the most creative places in the great city for the cyclist. Why? About halfway up the hill you get very tired, but what makes you feel even more tired is thinking about how far there is to go to the top and how much more tired you are going to feel before you get there. What you need to do is get your mind off the road and into something else.

'The mountain' is about using your problem or opportunity as a relaxing distraction from tough physical exertion, and as a way to generate brilliant ideas. The mountain is a demanding physical habitat, where you become acutely conscious of the 'struggle' that you are in the middle of.

The intensity of the immediate physical struggle allows your mind to become relaxed about the problem or opportunity for which you need the brilliant idea. It is this relative relaxation that loosens the mind to think freely. While you are truly challenged by the physical task you have undertaken, it offers mental respite, and this is useful in calming your mind, helping you to complete the demanding physical task and exploring ideas.

And, by the way, you're at the top of the hill now! Better stop and write down those brilliant ideas.

Why choose the mountain?

- The tension that was associated previously with trying to create brilliant ideas is temporarily delegated to the need to complete the physical task in hand. You become relaxed about the problem or opportunity goal.

- This relaxation creates the necessary mental conditions for great idea generation, as well as a healthy body and healthy mind – essential requirements for all fertile ideas habitats.

Summary

The implication in this chapter is that many of the mental habitats for brilliant ideas can be 'created' by you, and this is indeed true. However, there will be times when at least some of these habitats (the jungle, for example) will be the ones in which you need to survive through no fault of your own.

In either circumstance it is important to remember that you always have choices available to you. Perhaps the overarching lesson of this chapter is that there is much more that you can control about your surroundings than at first may seem to be the case. Create the conditions that are the best for you and the kind of person you are.

CHAPTER 3

Overcoming psychological barriers

Perhaps the biggest psychological barrier to generating brilliant ideas is self-inflicted. Many of us believe we are not creative. Life quickly becomes a self-fulfilling prophecy if we believe something strongly about ourselves because we then act as though it were true and we create that perceived reality. If we continue to behave as though it is true, we perpetuate the myth.

In this chapter we look at overcoming six psychological barriers that can prevent us from using our wonderfully creative minds to their greatest potential. These barriers are:

1 Being stuck in the mud – 'I am as I am'

2 Living in fear

3 Being 'in administration'

4 Having trouble with 'other people'

5 Becoming institutionalised

6 Overcoming personal constructs

Barrier 1 – Being stuck in the mud ('I am as I am')

Here is a test, and it comes in three parts. Please do each part in turn before reading and doing the next one. The whole test will take 10 minutes. You fail only if you don't have a go. Everyone who does it passes.

Take three sheets of A4 paper and some pens – lots of colours if you wish.

1   You are a shoe manufacturer and you have been invited to exhibit your new shoe at a footwear exhibition in Milan. Please draw a rough sketch of your latest design on the first sheet of paper.

2   You are a manufacturer of CD boxes, and a top record label has asked you to email a copy of your new design for a CD box. Please draw the design now on the second sheet.

3   A telecommunications company has asked you to design a mobile phone shaker. Please submit your design on the third sheet of A4 paper.

Well done – you've passed. Now let's see why. Have a look at your first two designs. You might have a few creative flourishes with these – a bit of colour and so on – but they will bear a strong resemblance to a shoe and a CD box, thus proving, you might say to yourself, that I am as I am. And if you believe you are not particularly creative, you might say that this belief has been proved.

Actually, what you have done is to prove that your ability to be truly creative is hampered only by previous knowledge and experience (in this case, of shoes and CD boxes). Indeed, the designs presented by everyone will be very similar. How do I know this? Because if I took all the designs of all the (millions!) of readers of this book of the mobile phone shaker, I know I would get a remarkably varied and creative batch of ideas. There would be a few similarities and some wonderful ideas. What is a mobile phone shaker? No one knows, and because you don't know, your thoughts are immediately liberated to create whatever you want.

One of the hallmarks of the 'I am as I am' mindset is to say 'I am not creative'. You are.

Barrier 2 – living in fear

Actually, I am being crafty with the exercise opposite because I know that some of you will have given up on step 3 of it precisely because you have no frame of reference for the mobile phone shaker. That doesn't mean you failed. It does mean you need to overcome your fear of stretching out or conquering lazy thinking. Let's look at some common reactions to fear of the unknown.

I can't do that!

While you might decide that there are limits on which ideas you put into action, there are no limits on your imagination or what you can think. A mobile phone shaker can be whatever you want it to be. The self-censorship and analysis can be saved for a later stage. You might say that your ideas are risky, but you can worry about the risk later. Meanwhile, there is no risk involved in thought.

I will look silly if I get it wrong

Nothing new ever came from anyone who worried that they might look silly. Today's silliness will be perfectly normal in the future. In medieval times 'silly' meant 'blessed'.

I can't see the point of change

Humans are innately conservative and aren't overly keen on change. And yet some might argue that what makes us unique among species is that we fashion change out of willing it rather than through evolution. You have to believe change to be a good thing in order to unblock your resistance to generating future-focused ideas that will change things.

I'll treat it as a joke

When we are afraid – or at least unsure or edgy – we often revert to humour as a way of relieving tension. Humour is a great force for creative idea generation. You can harness your unease to work for you by using humour to entertain and embrace the fanciful or novel. Humour works in other ways too. It relaxes the mind, and a relaxed mind is often a more creative one.

Barrier 3 – being 'in administration'

It may only be an accident that the characteristics of a company 'in administration' – tightly controlled, no innovation, little freedom – seem to apply to those who work in predominantly administrative roles. Even those in fairly senior positions often complain that their roles seem to be have been taken over by bureaucratic systems that limit their freedom of action.

If you are in an administrative, detail- or systems-orientated role, it can be hard to reconcile the administrative, process-orientated nature of your job with your desire to be innovative because:

● You say, 'There is no room for it in this job. There are too many barriers to innovative thought.'

● You might believe that the mental processes for creative and administrative thought are very different from one another.

However, these are false assumptions. Now begin to overcome this mindset by applying the following steps:

Step 1. Recognise that as soon as you start questioning whether you can or cannot do something, you immediately create a block for your most creative thoughts.

Step 2. Encourage creative thoughts with the assumption that you can do anything you want. If necessary, divorce yourself from the job as you see it in order to remove yourself from the process-orientated mindset. This is equally true for readers who don't work in administrative roles, but who find themselves adopting the process-orientated mindset too often.

Step 3. Which of your ideas motivates you the most? Which one genuinely excites you? It is your motivation to do something that will break down the barriers to creativity and action. If you are not motivated, you will see barriers where none exist. If you are highly motivated, there may still be barriers but the 'can do' spirit ofd motivation will make these barriers surmountable.

Trust your gut instincts. Do not attach yourself to ideas that do not or only partially excite you. And make sure that the dangling of the financial carrot is not the only excitement factor for you. Very few of us are motivated solely by money.

Barrier 4 – having trouble with other people

Do you think that work would be so much easier if you didn't have to deal with other people? You are probably not alone. Financial 'gatekeepers', for example, can often be the biggest irritant to the person who wants to champion a brilliant idea.

But the irritant can also be your greatest ally. The traditional 'blocking' functions – finance, personnel, other administrative departments – are there for a reason. Ideas need to be commercially focused and financially viable in a business context, otherwise they might become a personal indulgence that puts the company at risk. Administrators can kill off your idea early if they do not understand your concept or feel that the figures are badly thought through. Be your own idea's greatest champion by getting them involved early and making them feel part of the idea. And be aware that those in administrative roles are paid to ask questions first.

- Inclusiveness and consultation early on pay dividends in the long run because the early involvement of potential stakeholders makes them feel that they have something personally invested in the idea too.

- If you see other people as your problem, why not get them involved in the idea-generation process now? Present your idea and ask involving questions.

- People like the flattery associated with an invitation to voice an opinion, so ask them: 'What would you do...?' or 'How would you go about...?'

- Better still is to ask questions that show you have understood that others have needs. For example, 'I am planning to do xxx/researching the market for xxx. What would your department/customer, etc. need for it to work best?'

The closer someone feels to something, particularly when invited to have input, the more they will feel a sense of attachment and will champion it – and you.

As many have said in the past, seeing the world in terms of 'we' rather than 'me' better satisfies the wants of 'me'.

Barrier 5 – becoming institutionalised

The longer we work for an organisation, the more we are in danger of being taken over – 'institutionalised' – by the conventions of that organisation. Being a prisoner of convention rather than an escapee from it means being a victim of the institutional memory of the organisation. All this collective knowledge and wisdom is very important, but it can also restrict the field of creative vision because the starting point is totally historical. Ideas may become reactive rather than proactive in this type of environment. We may still have creative ideas, but dismiss them by telling ourselves:

'This is the way we always do it.'

'Our way is the best way. There is no other way.'

'The company doesn't do this sort of thing.'

'To challenge the status quo invites ridicule.' (And it's too much like hard work.)

'It worked before, so it will work again.' (It might – but it might well not.)

'We're known as the best in the business.' (You might be today, but what about tomorrow?)

In other words, our ability to think freely is compromised by our being part of an institution and taking on the characteristics of that institution in our thinking unquestioningly. Organisations, and therefore the individuals who work in them, may start to adopt a purely problem-solving mentality rather than being future-focused and creating new opportunities. A lack of future thinking creates a lack of dynamism that permeates individual thought. Ask yourself honestly: 'Is this true of me? Or of the organisation I work with?'

Generating brilliant ideas means allowing yourself to escape from that imprisoned perspective. Historical reference should be part of the remit for generating ideas, but should not be allowed to dominate or restrict your thinking. Banish convention from your thoughts – at least for a time.

Barrier 6 – overcoming personal constructs

How do you see the world? Clinical psychologist George Kelly once said, 'No one needs to be a victim of their own biography'. By that he meant: the way you are now will have been shaped in large part by your experiences in life (good and bad), your cultural conditioning, parental and peer influence, combined with some genetic inheritance. But your past doesn't need to define your future. Sounds obvious?

Kelly would not be remembered if that was all he said. One of his most important works related to what he called 'personal constructs'. These are great tools in helping you to understand how you see the world – in particular, how to make sense of the chaos we seem to live in. Our concern here is with constructs and creativity.

Kelly argued that, like scientists who believe there is one right, absolute answer, we try to see one true reality about life itself. Of course, we all have different perceptions of what that reality is – we formulate our own versions. These constructs (and we have many of them in relation to 'me and my world') are essentially bipolar: they have two 'opposite' poles. For example, pick three friends and find a way in which two of them are similar and the third different. You might say John and Davina are 'warm' people, whereas Sheila is 'shy'. 'Warm' and 'shy' are your two poles (though not opposites). Someone else might also use the word 'warm' to describe two friends, but use 'distant' for the third. We all have different constructs.

Our constructs do a number of different things. The first and most important is that they help us to make sense of what is happening in the world. However, the danger is that the more embedded our constructs or beliefs are, the less able we may be to let go of them. We hold on to the existing construct until the evidence for adopting a new and different view becomes overwhelming. Some people are more flexible, taking the view that 'My constructs are based only on information and experiences I have collected in my life up to now', and that 'My constructs can and will change'. In reality, most of us sit between these two extremes.

To be creative we need to 'loosen' our constructs so that the mind becomes free to see alternatives and to embrace rather than try to make sense of the chaos.

Constructs and brilliant idea generation

If you see your constructs as your only reality and your target in life – that is to say, the way you see the world is the one true, unchanging reality – you do not invite the possibility of an alternative view of the world. For idea generation this position is a disaster. Why is this?

- If you only ever look under the same stones, you will only ever see the same things. The kind of things that like living under that particular stone. You will never see the wondrous things that live under other stones.

- Your individual interpretation of the world might tempt you to say that yours is the only world. There are, of course, millions of worlds out there. Otherwise we would all be the same. Allow for the fact that you could be wrong and that what you think is the one absolute truth could also be wrong.

- Seeing things as bipolar allows us to form constructs more easily. But a key to idea generation is that we have to allow for vagueness, shades of grey, abnormalities and haze. Out of uncertainty come focus and clarity.

- Your interpretation of the world is an interpretation, not the interpretation, of the world. You need to remain open-minded to a wide variety of viewpoints and perspectives.

Summary

In the last two chapters we have looked at two different kinds of barriers to generating brilliant ideas, namely, the habitats and mindsets that block creative thought. With our mind now 'unblocked', we are ready to generate all those brilliant ideas.

CHAPTER 4

How to generate brilliant ideas

There are many myths about thinking creatively. When the words 'creative' and 'business' were originally linked together many turned away because the word 'creative' was usually associated with artistic pursuits, such as painting or music. Where the connection was accepted, 'creativity' was seen as something appropriate for marketing or research and development (R&D) departments, but maybe not for finance, personnel or other administrative functions. Now no one is in any doubt that creativity, idea generation and innovation should be close to the heartbeat of any successful organisation.

In the introduction we said that your brilliant idea can range from being 'brilliantly simple' – the smallest thing, to being 'simply brilliant' – something that comes along to change everything. Whether you are in a position to think 'large' or 'small' in your own organisation, generating brilliant ideas is a central part of your job no matter what you do. The key question is, 'How do I generate these ideas?'

In chapters 2 and 3 we looked at the kind of habitats that generate the best ideas and the positive mindsets that will help you to think in a more open, confident way. In Chapter 1 we suggested some catalysts that will challenge you to see your work and your organisation differently, thus creating the need to generate brilliant ideas. In this chapter we begin with five different types of idea (idea dimensions) that you can generate, starting with the most simple and progressing to the completely crazy.

The five dimensions of idea generation

1 Vanilla

2 Chocolate

3 Neapolitan

4 Paradigm shifts

5 The 'Pataphysical

These come with examples of how they can be used, and are followed by a number of practical generation tools that you can use across dimensions 2–5.

You can count how many seeds are in the apple. But not how many apples are in the seed.

Ken Kesey, author of
One Flew over the Cuckoo's Nest

Dimension 1 – vanilla

Our brain is capable of creating the most inventive ideas from the most random connections. However, most of us also like to keep things easy and avoid having to think too much about what we are doing. We prefer procrastination to acting now. We prefer to keep things the way they are rather than to change. This conservative streak serves us well. We do not need continual reinvention. If we did, many of the basic things that we do without question – driving a car, boiling an egg – would be subjected constantly to rigorous analysis and reappraisal, and we would never get to work in the morning. Maybe we wouldn't even make it out of bed.

I call these actions and ideas 'vanilla'. We do not need to add additional 'flavour' to our thinking because we have a ready-made solution that requires little thought.

What can we say about the vanilla dimension?

This is usually the instinctive realm for ideas.

Vanilla 'ideas' aren't really ideas at all. They are habits.

Vanilla habits are crucial in organisations. They are the cement that binds the whole organisation together. A simple habit might be the method by which we pay people at work – last day of the month, direct credit transfer.

But beware…

Vanilla habits can easily become the 'only way' – they are so ingrained that they can easily blind us to the possibility that there could be another way. Eventually vanilla habits need to be changed, and when we do change them the four other dimensions come into play. In fact, many vanilla habits were once new evolutionary or revolutionary ideas that are now the unquestioned norm.

Dimension 2 – chocolate

Chocolate ideas are evolutionary ideas. Generating them does not require huge leaps in your creative imagination. But they do need you to take a creative leap. The leap usually comes about where we make a connection between two like or similar things that share a number of characteristics. We apply our knowledge of one to help us solve the problem of the other, or to make the most of the new opportunity. Here are two examples of thinking in this way.

  **Motown – 'their version of your problem'**

In the late 1950s Berry Gordy, the founder of the global music phenomenon Motown Records, tried to work out how he could devise a process for developing hit records. Rather than following current music industry models, he looked to something of which he had considerable experience – the motor industry. Gordy had worked as a mechanic in Detroit (nicknamed Motor City because it was the home of America's automotive industry) and applied his knowledge of the tightly controlled car production process to establish the template for generating hit records in what became called 'Hitsville, USA'. As a result, Motown Records, the music factory of black America, was born.

You have a problem and you need a solution. Why not apply the Motown principle to your situation? How did other people solve their version of your problem?

● Have a look at what people do in different industries from your own.

● Observe different industry sectors that share many of the objectives you have – profit, public service – but may be doing it in a way you hadn't previously considered.

● Read industry magazines – and not just those relating to your own industry sector.

● Use your own experience of places you have worked before. Or use the experience of friends and colleagues. How were their versions of your current problem solved?

brilliant The play – 'linking the like or similar'

In the US College Bowl football final of 1981 Stanford took the lead
with four seconds remaining. Berkeley seemingly had no hope of winning
through conventional or legal means. Stanford knew this, so they and
many of the 100,000 crowd started celebrating. But several of the Berkeley
football team doubled as the Berkeley rugby team. They stunned Stanford
by starting to play rugby-style – within American football rules – and
scored a sensational winning touchdown just as the final hooter sounded.
The scorer had to sidestep the Stanford marching band, which had already
started its repertoire of victory tunes. With great ingenuity Berkeley created
one of the greatest sporting moments in history.

A great idea-generation technique is also one of the simplest. Just
as Berkeley did in sport, we make a 'link between the like'. We
don't always need the mind-expanding, creative solution.

● When looking for ideas – to solve problems or create
  opportunities – it can be helpful first to try to access the
  knowledge you or others have applied in similar situations.
  What knowledge and skills could you and your colleagues be
  using more of?

Why complicate things…?

● In their seminal business book of the 1980s writers Tom Peters
  and Bob Waterman came up with the landmark acronym KISS
  (Keep It Simple Stupid). The best answers are sometimes the
  simplest. What are you trying to overcomplicate?

● Peters and Waterman also used the expression 'Stick to
  the knitting', meaning 'Do the things that you do best or
  differently'. Sometimes organisations have pockets of simple
  excellence that other teams or departments could learn from.

● Just because something is already being done doesn't mean
  that it is not a brilliant idea. The brilliance in it comes from
  the application of an old idea, action or habit in a new or
  similar situation.

Dimension 3 – Neapolitan

Third-dimension thinking is multi-flavoured. Third-dimension thinking is freeform, requiring of you a willingness to make connections between things that, on the surface, do not seem to share any characteristics. Neapolitan thinking can be highly unproductive and frustrating. Unlike Neapolitan ice cream, which successfully combines three flavours, there are some flavours that just do not go together. You have to play and experiment to find out, but you have to be prepared for failure. Make a connection and you can change the world, or your own little bit of the world.

 **Data storage – 'linking the unlike'**

Still using paper or electronic means of storing all that data you are collecting? Well, things are changing. Japanese scientists have noticed that the genetic coding in DNA works in much the same way as digital data. Research teams have already managed to store data in bacteria. As bacterial species are extremely robust and long living, the data stored in them could last a million years. Their capacity for storage is massive – far in excess of any storage mechanism we use at the moment.

Just like the Japanese scientists, we sometimes have to make random connections through imaginative mental leaps to create ideas and opportunities. And sometimes when we make those leaps we find all kinds of connections we would not have found if the leap hadn't been made.

- Try to 'link the unlike' when more conventional idea generation methods are not bringing about satisfactory possible solutions.

- When you've brought the unlike together look for ways in which they are similar.

- Look outside your subject. What can you learn from people operating in walks of life different from your own? What could the town planner learn about street design from the brain surgeon who knows all the ruts, gulleys and alleys of the human brain? And vice versa.

brilliant Challenging assumptions

An African village needed a supply of healthy water, and the villagers knew that there was an untapped underground source. A well was quickly dug, but they reached an impasse when it was realised that they couldn't afford an energy source – electricity or a petrol generator – to pump the water out. The assumption they made initially was that the energy source had to be a conventional one. Then they realised that they had access to the most natural energy source in the world – children! By getting children to play on the village roundabout, which they connected to the pump, they created a new energy source for bringing water to the surface. They came up with a brilliant idea because they challenged their assumptions.

Challenging our assumptions, as the African villagers did, invites us to think about an old or existing problem in a completely new way by creating a different entry point to it.

- Ask what you are assuming about the problem goal – is it limiting your ability to produce new ideas?

- Even if your assumptions are right, update them – things rarely stay the same for long.

- It is an old statement but often a true one – those who assume often make an 'ass' out of 'u' and 'me'.

- As one person said, anyone can look for history in a museum, or architecture in an airport. The idea generator can just as easily do this the other way round. In our example anyone can look for a fuel source in a garage. The three-dimensional idea generator looked for a fuel source in a children's playground and found the most abundant one of all.

Dimension 4 – paradigm shifts

The phrase 'paradigm shift' was coined by the physicist Thomas Kuhn in his book *The Structure of Scientific Revolutions*. Paradigms are sets of rules that help us to understand our world. We have paradigms for everything from the structure of the working day to the workings of the internal combustion engine.

Paradigm shifts can exist very neatly in creative dimensions 2 and 3, but they also warrant a dimension to themselves. Paradigm shifts have one specific characteristic: when the paradigm shifts, everyone goes back to zero. What that means in the workplace is that when the paradigm shifts in your industry, all the previous habits, practices, norms and conventions run the risk of becoming obsolete. The very basic assumptions you make about the way you work become challenged.

Here are two paradigm shift questions:

● *What is it impossible to do in your industry?*

● *If it could be done, how would it fundamentally change the way your industry operates?*

These questions can be applied directly to you and your job:

● *What currently isn't possible in your own job, but, if it could be done, would make it easier or different?*

The purpose of these questions is to come up with answers and then work backwards – in other words, to make the seemingly impossible (under current norms) possible. Ultimately, it doesn't really matter if the answer is a paradigm shift or not. What you have done is to rethink what you do and generate ideas across the dimensions from simple improvements to true paradigm shifts.

Another trigger to paradigm shifts is to ask, 'If I were a new competitor, what might I do to compete?' We know that many paradigm shifts come from new kids on the block who have nothing invested in the old way and therefore nothing to lose.

It's much better to create the new paradigm yourself, but you may have so much invested in the old way (both intellectually and financially) that you do not see the possibilities inherent in the new way. This is known as paradigm paralysis – 'Our way is the only way'. Creating new paradigms means never being blinded by the old way.

 **brilliant** Examples of paradigm shifts

So far we have looked at paradigm shifts in theoretical terms. What do they mean in practice? Let's have a look at a few examples.

Swiss watches
This is the most famous of all business examples. Until around 1970 the Swiss had 90 per cent of the world watch market. Less than five years later their market had collapsed. Seiko and Texas Instruments had seen the new paradigm of time-keeping and it was the quartz watch. The irony was that the Swiss had invented the paradigm themselves.

Aeroplanes in warfare
The old paradigm of warfare was the massing of troops from opposing sides facing each other. The First World War saw the introduction of aeroplanes, and the Second World War saw their effective use. In between, the Guernica bombings had demonstrated the full horror of aerial bombardment. War would never be the same again.

Jobs for life in the public sector
Perhaps some of the biggest paradigm shifts in the workplace have occurred in the public sector. In previous times the idea of the public sector generating income through commercial operations, or that a job in the public sector was anything but a job for life, would have been alien. Not now.

Buying music
Chainstore music shops started to claim that people weren't buying music in the quantities they used to. But they were. The new paradigm of music buying was fast becoming the download. Some bands and musicians were even selling direct to fans and making their name without the use of record companies. The music industry is evolving in times of true paradigm shift.

The way we work
Prior to the Industrial Revolution, work and home life merged into one, with most work being done by hand and close to home. Jobs were largely agricultural or labouring. Along came industrialisation and the focus on efficiency, resulting in work having to be 'organised' at a central point. This became the new paradigm. Many of us are starting to live the latest paradigms of work – portfolio careers, home working, staggered hours, flexi-time and being permanently 'on call' through email and various handheld devices.

Dimension 5 – the 'pataphysical

'Pataphysicians are a group of people around the world – mainly in Paris and London – who encourage absurdist, nonsensical thinking (the redundant apostrophe in their name is an example of their nonsense). They create apparently pointless projects, one of which is to satirise all the other projects they are working on. They ask silly questions, such as, 'What if chalk were like cheese?' The thinking is random and crazy, but so is the thinking required to generate the next generation of ideas. Out of one generation's absurdity comes the next generation's normality.

Go back to the ice cream flavours of the first three dimensions. The innovative manufacturers Ben & Jerry have a flavour (Cherry Garcia) named after the rock musician Jerry Garcia. When they are assessing flavours and names they always ask, 'Is it crazy enough?' The crazy should be entertained at the core of the business. It could be what makes the difference.

The world is becoming a crazier place. The competitive battleground between organisations is crazier. The public sector works in a way that would not have been recognised 30 years ago. If we could look forward 30 years, we'd probably regard much of what we might see as 'crazy'. Look back 30 years – what do you do now that previous generations might have seen as crazy?

- Ask whether your 'idea' is crazy enough.

- What might you come up with if you escaped from reality? Once you've generated some truly crazy answers, ask how you might make some of them reality.

- Inject a bit of crazy into your paradigm-shift thinking. Inject a bit of crazy into dimension 3, linking the unlike. What might happen?

- Entertain the impossible.

- Watch a few episodes of *Monty Python* to get yourself in the absurdist mood!

So far in this chapter we have looked at five different dimensions of generating ideas, and seen examples of where they have been used. To complete the chapter we now look at four approaches to idea generation that can be used in any of those dimensions. The first takes us off quite literally to another dimension...

 **brilliant** *Doctor Who* – playing psychological judo

One of British television's most famous pieces of music is the *Doctor Who* theme tune from 1964. Although written by Ron Grainger, the greatness of the piece is really down to electronic music pioneer Delia Derbyshire.

The whole of the backing bass line for the piece comes from the plucking of one string once. There are no musical instruments involved. Delia Derbyshire took that one note, stretched it, contracted it, contorted it and manipulated it to create all the different changes we hear in this seminal piece of music. It was so different from anything heard before that Ron Grainger wanted Delia Derbyshire to be given a co-writer's credit. The BBC refused.

Beware the assumption that says that the simplest idea is also the most limited. Ideas take on a life of their own, often because we let our own creative imagination 'play' with them.

- What simple ideas do you have that you are ignoring because you have assumed that they are too simplistic?

- What ideas could you contort, manipulate, stretch or contract? What might they become?

- Grapple with the original problem or opportunity – engage in vigorous psychological judo.

- As human beings, we are always able to create something revolutionary out of (apparently) almost nothing.

 The Trabant – learning from history

The two-stroke engine fundamental to the Trabant car – symbol of East German otherworldliness – produced a noxious-smelling exhaust emission with nine times the CO_2 level of a VW Golf. The Trabant is seen as a bit of an historical joke. But not by a new generation of car designers, who have taken note of the 'duraplast' frame made from recycled materials and strengthened with waste cotton. An environmentally friendly blueprint for the construction of the car of the future was made in the most unlikely of surroundings over 40 years ago.

Are there lessons from history (such as the Trabant experience) that you are currently ignoring and that could provide a creative opportunity for you, your team, department or organisation?

Look at what you did in the past.

- What good things did you do that seem to have been dropped or forgotten for no obvious reason?

- Ask the same thing about your competitors. What industry standards have been lost, of which at least a few might fundamentally improve the way you do business?

- Many new kids on the block don't do much that is new; often they do what you do but with new energy. They may notice that you have dropped your standards because you have been around too long. What good stuff did you used to do that you have stopped doing?

- Henry Ford was wrong. History is only bunk if you are a slave to it. Many creative thinkers bring together ideas from past and present to create the future.

 Ideas from mistakes

In the late 1950s the American feminist movement sought a title other than Mrs or Miss to attach to women – one that didn't reveal what they considered to be their irrelevant marital status. The answer 'Ms' came about through a mistake. Sheila Michaels, a civil rights activist, received a letter with a typing error. It was addressed to Ms Michaels. From there was born the title that eventually became the mode of address for women who didn't want their name to indicate if they were attached to a man or not.

A cliché with much truth to it says that if you aren't making mistakes, you aren't trying anything. An extension of this says that in mistakes we often find an interesting path or diversion that would never have opened up if the mistake hadn't been made.

Ask these two questions:

● What's gone wrong for you?

● What hasn't gone the way you thought it would?

Then ask:

● In those mistakes are there interesting ideas and solutions that could be separated from the whole and developed?

● Can you take the 80 per cent of something that is good and rework the 20 per cent that isn't right and strengthen what you have? (Just because something doesn't work the way you imagined doesn't mean that it is all bad.)

Shopping and forests – what if?

The 'what if...' question is a classic tool for idea generation, and it can work as a catalyst in stages 2–5. There are two ways to ask it. The first is to ask straightforward questions, such as, '*What if we wanted to be the biggest company in the industry within five years?*' or '*What if we decided to offer a level of service superior to our competitors*', *regardless of cost?*' You then work through a variety of scenarios and ideas that might make those 'what ifs' a reality.

The second way to pose a 'what if...' question provides a great link into dimensions 3, 4 and 5. It brings together two previously unrelated concepts to see what can come out of them. A classic one has traditionally been: 'What if service was like being in love?' Answers include: 'Get close to the customer, show them you really care, listen to everything they tell you, make them feel special.'

Imagine you work in retail and you want to make shopping a bit more engaging. Link the word 'shopping' to almost anything and see what connections can be made. Here a connection is made between shopping and walking through a thick forest:

- Fresh smell
- Calming ambient noises, but no muzak
- Shafts of beautiful light
- Incredible activity, but barely noticeable
- Things to eat (free food?)
- Shelter, creating a feeling of being out of the rat race rather than in it
- Variety
- Lots of pathways (easy-to-follow walkways)

You can then use these ideas as catalysts for further idea generation.

Remember the following three rules when making links:

1 A connection must be between two unrelated concepts.

2 Don't choose a concept because it seems easy. The best connections often come from the most unlikely of partners.

3 Be truly random and playful with the connections.

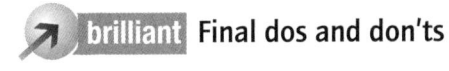 **Final dos and don'ts**

- Do remember that being creative is about generating brilliant ideas when we really need them.

- Don't jump on the first idea that arrives in your or somebody else's head. Being creative is about getting 'right' answers – and there are many right answers.

- Do continue to generate brilliant ideas when there may not be an obvious need for them.

- Don't evaluate your ideas too soon or you block the 'open' thinking required for brilliant idea generation. Assume that all answers are right answers. Save the judgement for later.

- Do be dissatisfied – there is far more to be created than has been created up to now. And the more we create, the more there is to create.

- 'Don't play what is there, play what is not there,' said the jazz great Miles Davis. Being creative is about finding space to move into – and then moving into it.

Summary

In the last three chapters we have worked on the process for generating brilliant ideas and making them happen. In the next chapter we move into Stage 3. You've got lots of ideas. Now is the time to be judgemental – to select the best and shape up each idea so that it's ready to reveal itself to the wider world.

STAGE 3

Decision-making

CHAPTER 5

People
challenges

Many of the answers to your organisation's future – in terms of product development, improved service offerings, innovation, brilliant ideas and true paradigm shifts – lie in the conversations that people have within your organisation. Future-focused conversations are taking place all the time in all organisations. You are having them yourself – either with yourself (in your head) or with colleagues. Brilliant ideas are the result of those conversations. Brilliant actions can be the result too.

You may have to fight with guerrilla tactics at one extreme to get your brilliant ideas taken on. You are likely to encounter resistance, personal vanity, other people's egos (and your own), as well as forms of protectionism, if what you propose fundamentally challenges the way people do things. It is amazing to see, for example, how protective people become of bureaucratic procedures that they themselves have criticised because a change will challenge the status quo. A natural fear of change and the unknown rears its head.

However, it is worth reminding yourself that you might need to give people time to adapt and catch up with your thinking. After all, they have not lived with your brilliant idea for as long as you have. Part of your role is to diffuse others' fears and to make them want the change you are proposing as much as you do.

This chapter could sit anywhere in this book because its lessons apply to all stages of the brilliant idea process. Although much of the text is addressed directly to you, rarely do we act in isolation, and other people will always be part of the mix. It is essential, therefore, that you establish the strongest relationships with those who are connected in any way to your brilliant ideas. People are an important variable. They are the key to your idea's success or failure.

The human mind likes a strange idea as little as the body likes a strange protein, and resists it with a similar energy.

William Beveridge,
social reformer

A kind of intelligence

Working with others requires a particular kind of intelligence. It requires you to know and understand yourself and it requires you to be able to dig deeply into the worlds of others so that you can understand them better too. You cannot bludgeon other people and expect your idea to be universally accepted. Your idea will work only if you learn that you get results through other people and not despite them. This sounds obvious, of course, but even though we know it, we rarely act on our knowledge.

This section describes the key personal traits required to champion an idea, and four key skills that will help you to look inside other people's worlds. You have to know and understand the worlds of others before you can expect them to want to understand yours.

Knowing yourself

This requires you to understand what/how you think, intuit, feel, believe and behave. Know your strengths and vulnerabilities. It is easier to understand other people's worlds if you understand your own.

Knowing others

In order to know others you have to get into and understand their worlds. Use the skills of questioning, listening and empathy to break down prejudicial barriers. These skills are examined in the pages following.

Controlling yourself

This means maintaining control of your thoughts, feelings, impulses and behaviour. It means controlling your emotions – a challenge when you are likely to be strongly emotionally attached to your idea. See Chapter 11 for more on this.

Motivating yourself

Keep yourself 'up' when you find yourself working with the most resistant of groups and individuals – and remind yourself that you have complete faith in your idea.

Working with others

Creating positive relationships where there is mutual benefit should be central to your thinking. In the context of your idea it also means motivating others so that they are as enthusiastic about your idea as you are.

> Have faith in your idea and the chances are that you can persuade others to have it too.

Empathy

*Empathy is the gift of showing you understand and care for
someone else's position.*

Tudor Rickards,
Creativity and Problem Solving at Work

Ignoring what people want, think, need, feel or believe in order
to get your way will work once. After that you may still get
agreement, but never commitment. Getting to know what others
truly want (and this is essential as you sharpen up your idea and
get commitment to it) means tuning in.

Tuning the radio

Imagine that you have an old wireless. It will take you some
time to adjust the dial to a point where you will get the right
wavelength for the station you want to listen to. It might take you
a bit of time, but you know it is worth it to get the tuning right.

● Getting to understand people and their needs and wants is
like this. We keep making small adjustments in our questions
and overall approach until we are in tune with their world.

Sometimes the station tunes out again and you need to fiddle
around with the dial until you get clear reception. Empathy is
underpinned by questioning and listening. And then questioning
and listening again. And if necessary again and again.

Drop assumptions

We all tend to categorise people in our mind or in conversation
because it makes them easier to understand. Most of us categorise
within the first five seconds of meeting someone. Some of us do
it before we even shake hands (by assessing the way someone
looks, dresses and talks).

Think about how you categorise people at work. Some stereotypes
include: 'Finance people are unimaginative and won't appreciate

new ideas.' 'Marketing people are creative and are therefore more open to new ideas.' 'Sales people are full of energy and will immediately put your idea into action.' 'Personnel departments are "blockers".'

Drop your assumptions about people. Take the finance team, for example. They might love your brilliant idea. What they won't love is the profit and loss sheet being last in your list of priorities – particularly if your idea costs money. Having a good friend in the finance department is one of the best allies you can have. Show finance people good and early that you care about their concerns and value their input, and they will care more about your idea. Always work in partnership with the person who controls the purse strings.

Ask the question – don't guess the answer

My mother made me a scientist without ever intending to. Every other Jewish mother in Brooklyn would ask her child after school: 'So did you learn anything today?' But not my mother. 'Izzy,' she would say, 'did you ask a good question today?'

Isaac Isidor Rabi,
physicist

Asking great questions will do two things for your brilliant idea:

● It will 'shape' your idea so that it more closely matches the needs of stakeholders, colleagues and your organisation as a whole.

● It will show you are interested in others (through your attentiveness to their needs and wants), making them more likely to show interest in you and your idea. Remember the old saying: 'Behaviour breeds behaviour'.

There are many types of question you can use, but the five types overleaf will be particularly useful both in shaping your ideas and in getting others involved.

Explorative question

This is an 'open' style of question that encourages a free and open response. For example:

> *'I'm trying to do x. What are the key issues for you?' 'How would this affect the work of your team/department/you?' 'What would you like to see happening?' 'How might this work for you?' 'What do you see as the challenges?'*

Sharing question

This is an open and collaborative style that implies shared ownership of the idea. For example:

> *'What do think we could do to overcome x problem?' 'I'm trying to do this. What would you do if you were in my situation?'*

Experience question

Similar to sharing, this too is an open and collaborative style, but tells the person you are speaking to that they have expertise that you lack or need. For example:

> *'In your opinion...?' 'You've had some experience of this.' 'Has anyone tried to do something like this before? What happened?'*

Clarifying question

This is a more closed style of questioning that invites a specific response to a specific issue. It may lead to the other styles of question above, but is used to test particular facts and details. For example:

> *'Can I be sure that I've got this right?' 'I just want to check I have understood you.' 'I'd like to ask you more about that specific point.' 'I want to check that I heard you right.'*

Summarising question

This is a statement rather than a question. It is designed to 'close the deal' and to ensure that you have shared understanding of the points discussed. If you can gain consensus at this point, you are more likely to get the person you are addressing to 'buy in' to your idea. For example:

'From what you've told me...' 'So the key issues for you are...'

Reminders

- Contrary to perceived wisdom, there is nothing wrong with the closed question that gets a 'yes' or 'no' response – as long as a 'yes' or 'no' is what you seek.

- The best questions are the ones that connect what you want to say to the other person's world.

- Remember to make regular use of the other person's name, particularly if you don't know them well. It emphasises your personal connection and shows them that you care about their response.

Listen

Asking questions is step one in the process of establishing relationships and getting wider involvement and commitment to your idea. Step two is to listen to others and to listen especially closely to the answers to your questions. Much is written about listening and the difference between 'active' listening and 'passive' listening. Good questioning and listening should enable you to get out of your own mind and into the mind of the other person. Empathic, projective and transportive are good words to describe the listening process.

● Maintain 'interior curiosity'. Be curious about what's going on inside the other person rather than focusing on the exterior.

● Listen with the intent to understand rather than with the intent to respond immediately. As soon as we start to prepare a reply in our mind we stop listening because at that point we are talking to ourselves instead.

● Leave feelings about the other person aside as they will cloud the neutral stance you need to take.

● Hold back. It is so easy to jump on the first thing we agree or disagree with and thus deny ourselves the whole story. If you have a view, avoid stating it too soon otherwise the conversation becomes biased to your view rather than being a proper search for the views of the other person.

● Try not to relate everything the other person says to your own world. Inevitably, you will do so eventually because you might need to adapt your brilliant idea to accommodate the views of that person. However, do this too soon and you will fail to explore the mind of the other person. You might miss out on problems you hadn't thought of, or possibilities you hadn't seen.

Remember, this is not the time to massage your ego by suggesting 'Aren't I brilliant for thinking of this?' This is the stage where you test the validity of your idea and do your research.

Prejudice or pre-judgement

All of us manifest prejudice at some time or another – it is part of being human. Prejudice means to pre-judge or to make assumptions about people because of what or who they are. We all do it, no matter how hard we try not to.

Beware of your own prejudice when in brilliant idea mode because it leads to self-imposed barriers to progress. For example, ask yourself whether you ever assume that certain individuals or groups cannot do certain things, or will do things in a certain way because of the characteristics you associate with that person or group. Pre-judging them may also lead you to exclude them as suitable idea accomplices. As a result, you might overlook someone who could become a great ally and champion of your idea.

Nobody changes prejudicial views as a result of reading a few lines in a book because our prejudicial thinking comes predominantly from years of cultural conditioning. However, we can at least recognise and challenge our people judgements and value a breadth of contribution.

- See each person as a free consultant who can help shape, improve, freshen up and enliven your idea.
- Seek multiple perspectives. The more you seek, the more robust your idea will become. Are your perspectives all from similar kinds of people or groups?
- Even if you don't agree with the fresh perspectives, your challengers will allow you to wrestle with your idea and make it stronger.
- People 'not like me' provide a great test for your idea. People 'like me' will probably agree more easily to an untested idea.

Your idea will have greater credibility if it has a breadth of support. It will be a better and stronger idea for going through this testing process, just as research and development benefits from it in a wide variety of fields. We need to identify the weaknesses just as much as we need to champion the strengths. This is not an argument for tokenism – 'We need the views of someone who is from an ethnic minority', for example; nor is it an invitation to design by committee. Ask others for their views because you value and need their experience and expertise. It is the right thing to do both practically and commercially.

Reactions

People will probably respond to your idea in a variety of ways, so be prepared for their differing reactions.

Negative feedback

Not everyone is going to love your idea. You need to learn to receive feedback objectively, not personally. Remember, they are judging the idea, not you. Many of us are all too quick to give negative feedback, but find it much harder to take. Here are some tips for handling feedback:

● Remember, you should ask for it anyway.

● Thank the giver.

● Seek specific information – feedback is often given in general terms.

● Clarify where necessary.

● You do not have to agree, but don't argue or seek to justify yourself.

● Listen and understand.

● Is there a pattern emerging? Have others said similar things? If so, you are receiving useful information.

● Don't ignore it. Ask if you can use it.

Leaking

What people say and what people are thinking may not be the same thing. Sometimes they nod or say yes to show they are listening and have understood, rather than to show they agree with you. There is no point in getting the nodding head agreement and the positive words if they are merely masking discomfort at your idea. The affirmation will not be followed up by action or support.

Fortunately, we are not very good at hiding what we really think. We 'leak' the signals. For example, our body language may be 'uncomfortable' or ever-changing. We avoid eye contact. We may start to touch parts of our face regularly. We may speak in a more truncated form and lose conversational fluency.

This is where we need to 'retune the radio' back to the wavelength of the other person (see page 66). Revert to using the searching questions outlined earlier in this chapter. Invite direct comments. (Sometimes people worry that they might cause you personal offence.) Explain that future problems could result if they agree now to something they are not happy about. If necessary, explain your own frustration if you sense unease and a lack of transparency.

Nobody wants to know!

Ask yourself, why don't people want to know about your idea? It could be down to the organisational culture; it could be that you're not putting your point across effectively; it could be that you're working too much in isolation and no one has bought into the idea. It could also be that it is a great idea, but that its time is not now.

Sometimes we can find our ideas being met by a wall of silence. You might work with people who do not even perceive the need for brilliant ideas.

brilliant We gotta problem...

'I fell into a vat of chocolate,' sang one of the comic duo the Smothers Brothers. 'What did you do?' asked the other. 'I shouted, "Fire!",' sang the first. 'Why?' 'Because I figured that if I shouted, "Chocolate!" no one would notice.'

Like the inventive Smothers brother above, if you want to highlight a problem, you sometimes need to be creative in the way you do so. What can you do that will make people stand up and take notice?

The Jonathan Ive approach

In some circumstances people might be glad that you have a potential solution to a problem. They will be relieved that they do not have to think about creating a solution themselves. The advice in this instance is to present your idea as if the solution is simple. Jonathan Ive, who leads the Apple design team that produced the iMac, iPod and iPhone, said about his co-workers:

'We try to solve complicated problems without letting people know how complicated they are.'

This is another way of saying 'Here's a problem and here is a simple solution'. You can let this person know that we are not passing all our problem stress over to them after all and they will be mightily relieved about that and more accepting of a simple solution. This approach works well with people who retreat into their shells when a big problem comes along. However, it should not be seen as a cheap way of pushing ideas through without sensible discussion.

Jonathan Ive has more excellent advice for those who are tempted to parade their ego alongside their idea – another reason why you might get the 'underwhelming' reaction.

'The design we practise isn't just about self-expression. I don't want to see a designer wagging his tail in my face. I want to see a problem solved.'

Influencing strategy

In most instances you will find you need to be able to influence others before winning them over to your brilliant idea. We have suggested several of the interpersonal qualities you will need, including questioning, listening and empathy. There are also a few other strategies that you can use to influence the decision-makers.

Your reputation

Knowing that you have experience and a good reputation in your field is very reassuring to others. Using your reputation as a strategic tool needs to be done with great sensitivity, as you don't want to upstage or threaten anyone. Usually, however, having a good reputation is a definite door opener.

Reason

We are reasonable people if treated reasonably, and most us can see reason if it is presented to us. Some brilliant ideas are simple, sensible methods for dealing with long-standing problems. In these instances sensible, logical well-thought-out arguments may be the most influential and likely to 'win the day'.

Trust

Identify the people with whom you have good, long-standing working relationships. These are probably the people that you most trust within the organisation. Trust among colleagues is born out of a combination of respect, knowledge and previous success. However, beware of 'using' previously good relationships to gain credence for your new idea. The danger is that people may sense that the trusting relationship is being manipulated. Emphasising common ground is the best way around this. Can your idea benefit all parties concerned?

There are also two more 'political' possibilities available to you for influencing others.

Coalition forces

If your idea needs approval from higher up, there can be strength in numbers. Bring together a team to present your idea.

Bargaining

'If you help me on this, I owe you one...' With those we know well, a bargain might be implied rather than clearly stated. Good relationships at work depend on helping each other out. But where you have to explicitly offer a 'trade', beware being overly beholden to someone in the future.

Summary

As someone once said (only partly in jest), living would be so much easier without other people around. Some might say the same about work too. Undoubtedly, people will present the biggest barrier in getting your idea accepted and actioned if you don't adopt positive approaches to colleagues. On the other hand, strong working relationships can be the very thing that catapults your brilliant idea into successful action. Here's a quick reminder of things to do and to avoid when developing those valuable relationships.

- Do seek a deep understanding of the worlds of other people.
- Don't treat workplace relationships lightly.
- Do make other people the genuine centre of your attention.
- Don't try to manipulate others to your way of thinking.
- Do give with no expectation of something in return.
- Don't just ask, 'What's in it for me?'
- Do treat the workplace as a research laboratory for mutually beneficial ideas.
- Don't deflect attention away from yourself or avoid responsibility when there are problems.
- Do ask good questions and listen well.
- Don't ignore the risks.
- Do invite feedback, both good and bad.
- Don't sell your soul to the devil to get what you want.

CHAPTER 6

Ideas in the lab – the hard tests

We are now well into the third stage of the brilliant idea process, and it is likely that you are by this time collaborating with other interested parties who are getting closely involved with your ideas. In fact, the bigger the idea, the more closely involved the other potential stakeholders should be with what you have in mind.

If your idea is small scale, or relates only to the functional detail of the work you are doing, you may be working in a degree of isolation, or with just one or two people. However, many of the techniques described in this chapter can be used whether you are working towards an individual or a collective decision about the future of your idea.

Futurologist Joel Barker once pointed out that intuitive judgement means making good decisions with incomplete data. In fact, every decision we make needs a large slice of intuitive judgement because if we waited until we had complete information, we would never have enough to take action. As writer Edward De Bono tells us, if we had complete information to get the right decisions, we wouldn't need human beings to make them. In other words, if decisions were made with complete data, computers could make them without any need for our input.

> Every decision we make needs a large slice of intuitive judgement because if we waited until we had complete information, we would never have enough to take action.

Therefore, all decision-making is largely an intuitive process (but this is not the same as saying it is emotional). This chapter explores the different analytical techniques we can use to come to good decisions – what we might call the 'hard tests'. In the next chapter we investigate the softer side of decision-making, which includes an analysis of how we can use intuitive 'feelings' – individually and collectively – to make good decisions.

Analytical 'hard' tests include:

- First tests
- Market evidence
- Resources
- Information
- Group assessment

First tests

There are four very clear questions that should be asked at the beginning of any decision-making process. These relate to the following factors:

1 Pressure – is it a 'hot' decision'?

2 Importance – is it a key decision?

3 Priority – should I be allocating lots of time to this now?

4 Goal-scoring – does it meet the problem-solving or opportunity-taking goal?

1. Pressure – 'hot' or not?

Is the need for a decision about your idea essential now? How 'hot' is it? Are you operating in a crisis? Is the problem big, requiring an immediate solution? Is the opportunity going to be around for only a very short period of time?

There is a common tendency within companies to use crisis management techniques for making decisions in a non-crisis situation when a more considered approach might yield both better ideas and better decisions.

2. Importance – is it a key decision?

All decisions assume a level of importance. Typically, we agonise over making the 'right' decision in a situation where any number of possible decisions can be the right one, and are very good at getting bogged down in decisions about minor details. (For example, which colour to use on a book jacket, or what style of seats to book for a conference hall.) At this level it is our positive attitude about the decision that will dictate its success or failure. The greater the combination of pressure and level of importance, the higher the demand for more facts to support our decision. Yet the greater the urgency and pressure, the less likely we are to have all the facts. Indeed, too many facts can lead to hesitation and further delay in decision-making. The opportunity may pass, or the problem may grow much bigger. Trusting your instinctive 'feel' for the right decision becomes even more important under pressure.

3. Priority – now's the time?

Time is always a function of priority. Decision pressure and decision importance must shape your time priorities. Many of your brilliant ideas may not be priority 'now' decisions; they may still be important decisions, but they do not need to be made straight away. This is a good thing. Slower processes in decision-making can allow time for your intuition to work properly, resulting in a better decision about which direction to take. The hot priorities – where the decision must be made now – must be given precedence over everything else. Hesitation through excessive information gathering or fear of making the wrong decision can be fatal.

4. Is it goal-scoring?

In deciding which idea(s) to run with, you need to ask yourself, 'Does the idea meet the problem-solving or opportunity-taking goal?' For this purpose you can begin by rejecting all those ideas that do not do this. They may be useful elsewhere; indeed, they may be 'brilliant ideas' in their own right, so keep them in mind for possible use in another context.

Decision-making criteria

After the first tests we then move on to use some (or all) of the 'hard' analytical tools available to us in practical decision-making:

● Evidence of the market

● Resources

● People

● Information

Evidence of the market

Gathering market research is an important – sometimes crucial – aspect of developing products or services. It can often prompt our awareness of problems and opportunities in the marketplace that trigger our new and brilliant ideas. It is not the role of this book to look at research techniques, but it may be useful to note some warning signs about the excessive use of research.

● Be wary of small-scale market surveys, particularly if the selective evidence reinforces your own preferred viewpoint. One person's view, or a trial that involves only a few people, will be unrepresentative.

● Market research is rarely objective. It has often been commissioned by a commercial organisation aware that you sometimes have to lead customers rather than have them lead you.

● Research can mean that we give only what people want now because the customer base may reflect just the current market and not be forward-looking. Does the decision need to be future-focused or are we just looking after the present?

- The collective will of the current market may be less open than your imagination – why will people want what you are offering? Will the market have moved on by the time you launch your idea?

- Market research follows rather than leads the market, and, as a result, often leads to the development of lowest common denominator products and services.

It is important to keep your idea constantly in mind when you target your research so that you ensure you can connect your research findings to your original objective.

- Markets only really grow when someone or something comes along that surprises them.

- Are you happy to launch your idea within the existing marketplace or are you looking to create a new one (or both)?

- Pay attention to what some of the smallest, newest players are doing. They may be naive and hopelessly wrong in their approach, or they may be naive and so right that they are creating a new market paradigm.

- Sales people are often an excellent but ignored source of market information.

- Market research means not just exploring your customers' existing world, but creating entirely new worlds too.

If your idea is a true paradigm shifter or verging on 'crazy' (see page 53), there may be little market evidence to support its viability. The danger here is that the use of limited market evidence may compromise its potential; the originality and brilliance of the idea may be lost or overlooked in a desire to 'play it safe' and 'not make a mistake'. It is worth remembering that the most ground-breaking ideas succeed with little or no evidence or information to support their development.

Resources

Bear in mind that resources are precious and protected closely (and rightly) by those responsible for them. The examination of available resources is therefore essential in good decision-making. The obvious ones, such as finance and existing physical resources, need to be factored in here, but so does the most precious and most-abused of all resources – time.

Finance

The hardest of hard tests is the profit and loss sheet. Can you afford it? Will it be profitable? Some ideas cost almost nothing. Others require a lot of initial investment and take time to make a profit. Cash flow can make or break a company, so it is important to get the financial details right at the outset.

Most people recognise the value of empowering and developing people at work, and the need for flatter, less hierarchical organisations. There are also those who believe that the key to true commercial success lies in the ability of a handful of very sharp operators to move money around (legally, of course) in the right way. This has created a dominant 'bean-counting' mentality that pervades the culture in many organisations.

If developing your idea is likely to have a financial impact, you should already have your answer to the 'Can you afford it?' question. As we explored in Chapter 5, the early involvement of finance and other contributing departments will be absolutely essential in getting your idea accepted and actioned. Financial commitment is needed before any decision to proceed is made.

Knowing your profit margin and understanding the size of the investment required to launch your idea are invaluable factors in decision-making. The best ideas are the ones that have been costed and agreed by the finance team, and 'bought into' by the sales and marketing departments. Anything that doesn't meet the financial criteria should be dropped. Anything that doesn't have the full commitment of the sales and marketing teams might as well be dropped.

Treat your colleagues as you would customers. All internal financial agreements and sales commitments should be made in writing and signed off before the decision to develop the idea is acted upon. This encourages commitment – to the concept and to taking action to make it work.

Physical resources

IT, equipment and logistical support come under the umbrella of physical resources. All these cost money, so the same principles apply here as to finances (opposite). Being in line with your organisation's environmental policy and monitoring your carbon footprint might be factors too. The availability and cost of physical resources to support the idea will be key to your success.

Time

One of the most precious of resources is time. Even the smallest of ideas will consume time. Questions to ask before signing off on your idea are:

- Is the idea going to be compromised because of lack of time?

- If the idea is a big one, is everyone aware of the time implications? Has it been properly planned and costed? Are the resources available to manage the project effectively and keep it on time and on budget?

- If the idea is a small one, will the time spent actioning it justify the possible outcome (i.e. lots of time for only a small gain)? If not, choose not to take your idea forward. Small-scale ideas often take the same amount of time as large-scale projects to make them a success. They must be planned with care if they are to be viable.

- Problem-solving ideas might be needed more quickly and prioritised ahead of those that exploit new opportunities. Has sufficient time been allocated for the development of both kinds of idea?

People

Please note that people are not 'human resources' – they are human beings with all the brilliance, unpredictability and resistance to change that makes them human. Before you decide to move ahead with your brilliant idea there are several key questions to be discussed at this stage:

- How are those affected by your idea likely to view the change that it will bring?

- Is resistance to your idea likely to compromise it to such a degree that the idea will lose its impact?

- Does the long-term importance of your idea outweigh short-term human considerations?

- How much consultation with other departments should there be at this stage?

- How can I incorporate some of the ideas of those affected so that the idea becomes stronger and the acceptance of it greater?

A couple of points from Chapter 5 bear repeating here.

Never underestimate human resistance to new ideas. We don't like change very much, especially if it is forced upon us. On the other hand, a decision should not be taken just because it is the easiest in human terms. Decisions and actions often require a degree of bravery. That doesn't mean riding roughshod over colleagues – we should always be aware of likely reactions, and have plans thought through for meeting those reactions (see page 72). Most of all we need to be patient. An idea that we have lived with for months will be new to those who have heard it only once. Others need time to live with the thought and to assimilate their feelings about the change the idea will bring.

Never underestimate the impact of consulting early with affected groups. This allows them to feel that they 'part own' the solution rather than having it imposed on them.

We are human beings...

...but not necessarily human doings. It can be frustrating when people don't see the world from your perspective and can't show the same enthusiasm for your idea that you have. You may need to play a deeper psychological game and plant yourself into their 'world'.

You must understand that others will be looking at your idea from their perspective rather than yours. When making decisions, the human factor is critical because it is human beings and their commitment that will determine whether or not your idea is successful.

Decisions inevitably involve others, and when others become involved they may want to reduce the possibility of risk, reasoning that if the idea fails, they may be implicated. This is a cynical view, but one that underpins much of the decision-making that goes on in organisations, not least because we live in an age when everyone is dispensable and redundancies are an everyday occurrence.

Remember the fear factor in Chapter 3? Fear is a surprisingly common driver in the workplace. A need to safeguard themselves and prepare excuses in case of failure drives some people to require a wealth of information before committing themselves to taking action. This is a natural human reaction. In the case of the biggest ideas, careers and livelihoods may be at stake if things don't turn out as planned.

Information

The way we use information in decision-making is just as important as the amount of available information we have to support that decision. In this section we look at the questions we need to ask ourselves when using that information.

Reality check

How much information do you have in support of your ideas? In an information age dominated by the use of email, it can be hard to filter out the poor-quality data that contaminates good decision-making. Ask yourself whether irrelevant information is clouding the really important issues. Is your idea 80 per cent good and 20 per cent bad? That's fine. Use information that points to weaknesses to address the 20 per cent that needs improving, but don't drop the 80 per cent that is good!

Emotional contamination

Attachment to your idea is natural, and the 'heart' you have invested in your idea will, given half a chance, propel it to success too. It can also blind you to the weak spots in the idea, or lead you to ignore information that indicates it would be unwise to proceed. Many people stick blindly to their idea beyond the point where all logic tells them to stop. Ideas require hard-headed realism as well as emotional attachment. Separate yourself from your idea for a time and ask how others might see it.

Weight

Not all sources of information carry the same weight – we attach greater credibility to some than others. Imagine that you are considering moving the office computer system from PC to Mac. Whose expertise would you attach the greatest weight to? People who use both operating systems, your IT department, technical writers, friends or specialist Internet forums?

Less weight might be attached to those who are heavily in favour of one system (and are therefore biased), those who use a computer simply for typing letters and sending email, or perhaps those at a senior level whose administrative tasks are performed by others. The information might still be confusing and you might decide to trial the new system with a small group to see how they like it.

Information pollution

In this situation a clear distinction has to made between the use of supporting information that will inform the best decision, and the excessive use of information that will bog down the whole decision-making process. Information pollution kills the energy and life that were previously an intrinsic part of the idea.

The group decides...

If your idea has a wide impact on the organisation, it is highly likely that the decision-making process will be done by a group – usually consisting of those whose work will be affected by the decision.

The challenge of group decision-making is to avoid situations where a consensus view is reached without energetic discussion, probing questions and serious debate around the decision to be made. Compromise can often be made at the lowest common point among the group. This process is commonly described as 'group think' and often leads to a decision that no one has any objection to, but that no one feels passionate about either.

Poor group decision-making is particularly prevalent:

● Among people who have worked together for a long time, because the longer we are with people, the more likely we are to think like each other.

● In long-established organisations, where attachment to the 'old way' is more deeply ingrained.

● Where individuals lack the confidence to speak out.

● Where a dominant senior manager/leader figure is present and inhibits the voices of more junior colleagues.

● When attempting to decide what to do about a long-standing problem.

● Where idea generation has been over-controlled and only a few good ideas have been bought into during the decision-making phase. This occurs when too many voices (or a dominant voice) have been saying 'Yes, but...' as in '...but we can't do it', '...but xxx won't like it' and '...but we tried that years ago'.

Passionate debate delivers the best results and turns good ideas into brilliant ones. It ensures all aspects of your idea have been tested with the full rigour of contrasting opinion. Ideally, have someone other than you to lead that debate. You need someone who will not express an opinion, but who is able to get others to do so. A good idea will easily stand up to the push and pull of strong debate. You need to be ready to play devil's advocate if there is no constructive disagreement emerging.

brilliant Key points in group decision-making

As we have seen, several of the processes involved in making decisions connected to your brilliant idea can be used alone or in groups, and some of these are summarised below. However, some are unique to groups, and these are highlighted with an asterisk (*). You will find many of these suggestions particularly useful in breaking through the problem of group-think consensus decision-making highlighted on the previous page.

1   Wrestle with the ideas.

2   There should be dissent, disagreement and 'friendly' conflict.*

3   Encourage everyone to voice their inner thoughts. There is no point in having agreement if there is unexpressed disagreement.*

4   Although the pathway to agreement may seem smooth, any disagreement kept bottled up will manifest itself in the action stage – the worst time possible for your idea (and the most costly).*

5   No decision will be perfect. Far better to be honest about shortcomings and risk now because these can be addressed as you move into the action stage.

6   Do not strive for perfection for its own sake. Perfection is about stasis, whereas creativity and success require flexibility and a willingness to change. The pursuit of 'perfection' will inevitably lead to paralysis and idea death.

7   It is particularly important to encourage the quieter members of the group to speak out. They may have a valuable contribution to make to the discussion but, for whatever reason, have chosen not to, or find it hard to voice their opinions.*

It may feel strange to use these tactics to argue against yourself, but it may be necessary to do so. However, don't become a martyr and provide too much rope to hang yourself with.

Reasons and feelings

In decision-making, information gets you only so far; a separate process – the use of 'inner feeling' or what some call intuition – takes you the rest of the way. Below is an exercise taken from my book on opportunity-spotting and taking (*Make Your Own Good Fortune*), which highlights the link between some of the 'harder' processes (your experience, for example) and some of the 'softer' processes (intuition, 'heart') that are at play in the making of good decisions.

 **The waiting game – a decision-making exercise**

Imagine you are a card player. You are playing a poker game and the stakes are high. You think you hold a winning hand (the great opportunity) but you are considering some of the options open to you. Think about what those options might be:

● You could play your hand now and not benefit from the gains you would have made had you held your potentially winning hand for longer.

● You could save yourself from a big defeat later on for a smaller gain now. Less risky, but you miss out on the big win.

● Or you could opt for a less rational decision-making process that relies on your instinct to show your hand at exactly the right moment.

What would you use to try to make the best decision?

Experience: What worked in previous situations like this? Or is this the first time you've ever played the game? Remember, though, that no two situations are alike.

Probability: What is the likelihood that other people hold better hands? Again your previous experiences might play a part.

Intuition: This means you have a feeling that your hand is better than anyone else's. Can you get a 'feel' of the mood from the clues that others are sending out?

Head and heart: Don't let the excitement of the moment mean that your emotions run away with you and distract from your rational, more measured side. The best decisions need a combination of head and heart: 'whole... heart...head' (or 'wholehearted'). Can you control your emotions to the extent that you don't reveal your pleasure at what you think is a winning hand? Can you control your emotions to the extent that you choose when to make your decision and avoid making a bad one? Controlling heightened emotion may lead to better decisions and greater rewards. It may also help you to act at the right moment rather than at the moment when impulse overwhelms you.

Opportunity: If I don't take the opportunity now, would I ever act? This is a great chance for me. I must not let myself become so obsessed by doing the right thing that I become paralysed into doing nothing.

Summary

In this exercise we have seen the connectivity between the hard and soft tests.

In the next chapter we look at the soft side of making brilliant idea decisions.

CHAPTER 7

Ideas in the lab – the soft tests

If you make a decision at work and try to justify it by saying, 'It feels right', you might not be taken seriously. And yet, in reality, many of our decisions are made with a large dose of this 'gut feeling'. Of equal importance to success is the commitment we give to the decision once we have made it. Commitment is an emotional response, and even with the 'hard' analysis we looked at in Chapter 6 (based on market research, facts and others' knowledge), our emotions are going to be the strongest force in making our decision and then acting on it.

In this chapter we examine the emotional element in decision-making, and, in particular, the use of intuition.

What is intuition?

Intuition is a sensory process that moves us from position A to position B because in some way it 'feels' right. It plays a critical role in decision-making. Information can help us to start looking in a certain direction but it is intuition that will propel us forwards. Successful use of intuition is an emotional mechanism that helps us to make good decisions. When we use it we are really saying:

'This decision feels more right than the others.'

Intuition has been described as a 'me inside myself' feeling. It works best when it combines all the critical decision-making factors – experience, knowledge, relevant information – with a sense of 'this is the time', commitment to the idea, engagement with the original problem or opportunity, and also self-confidence.

> Intuition and gut feeling are one and the same thing.

East versus West

Those who champion the use of intuition in business suggest it is one of the deepest thought processes of all because it combines experience, information and your deepest feelings and knowledge about something. In Western business culture there is a prejudice against being seen to make decisions that rely upon intuition, even though, in reality, it nearly always plays an important part.

When companies acquire other companies they will often release the hard information about costs, synergies and head-count. But they will also release the softer information that informed their decision about 'good fit', the 'feel' of the acquired business and so on. This isn't just for the benefit of the staff of the newly acquired business. It will have informed the business decision substantially, unless the reason for buying was that the acquired business was going bust or had asset-stripping potential.

Why intuition can work for us

● Intuition might work for us because we feel we strongly 'own' the idea or the decision: it has come from the deepest part of our psyche. Ownership of the concept keeps us personally close to it and therefore provides the emotional propulsion to make the right decision.

● Intuitive decisions might suit the kind of person you are. Perhaps you naturally work along the lines of: 'If it feels right, I am more likely to be committed to action'.

● Knowing that your intuition has worked in the past will increase your personal confidence. Having confidence that we can 'get it right' gives us a belief in our decision-making powers. That belief can be very important.

● In the end great decision-making combines both intuition and the logical, rational use of information. Don't let the endless search for information paralyse you when it comes to making a decision. But, on the other hand, don't let intuition prevent you from searching for relevant information to support your idea.

● Intuitive thought is far more knowledge- and experience-based than people realise. If it weren't, our intuitive feelings would never change. Intuitive responses to an identical set of circumstances would be very different at the age of 20 compared to the age of 40.

● Intuition can be highly directive. At a fork in the road it can lead us down a more rewarding path.

Perhaps even more important than knowing how intuition can work for us is knowing when and how it can let us down.

Where intuition can fail us

● Intuition is an emotional process and might not help us to make wise decisions when we are overly attached to an idea. In other words, we see what we want to see and ignore the things we don't want to or are blind to – perhaps because it is inconvenient to do otherwise.

● Intuition can breed arrogance. The belief than one is always right precludes the possibility of using previous bad experiences as a learning opportunity. We know that experience fine-tunes intuition. Arrogance can make us ignore contradictory evidence.

● Intuition cannot tell the time. Sometimes it works quickly, sometimes slowly, and sometimes we have no intuitive feeling at all about a right course of action. If there is no pressure to make a decision immediately, do not do so. Give your mind time to work. If you have no intuitive feeling for the right decision when under pressure (and, of course, for some of us pressure can actually sharpen the intuitive feeling for the right course of action), you must rely on the information you have, or just make any decision at all and commit to it wholeheartedly.

● Intuition should not be confused with false hope. There are people around the world who have spent their whole life pursuing something unquestioningly because powerful emotional drivers within them compel them to do certain things. They go disastrously wrong because their driver is false hope rather than intuition.

● It seems strange, but those with a highly optimistic disposition may also see intuition failing them. Optimism of the 'Everything will be all right' kind means that crucial experience and knowledge may not be fully absorbed, making intuition less 'informed' as a result.

Making intuition work

You are looking your brilliant idea in the face. You are trying to make the decision about whether and how to proceed with it, and you are needing a large dose of intuition to help you. How do you make intuition work for you?

● Flick a coin to make a decision. Are you pleased with the result or did you secretly hope for a different one? This approach can be useful if you are struggling to tune in to a decision. It can be used in groups too.

● Put the decision in your mind, shut your eyes and blank out all the thinking connected with that decision. The residue, the feeling you have, is your gut feeling. This is a tougher technique to use, and it is likely that you will need some sort of diversion (such as sport or reading something unconnected to the topic in hand) so that you can blank out thoughts related to the decision.

● Using your imagination, place each of your possible decisions behind a separate door. If you have any decisions to make at the moment, do this now. Then look at each of the doors closely. Which ones are shut and which are open? Discount the shut doors. Pick the door that is open the widest. Behind that door is your preferred decision.

> Intuition should not be confused with false hope: that can lead to disaster.

Intuitive groups

Groups can also be intuitive, but their intuition needs to be based on the evidence of the hard tests that are described in Chapter 6, otherwise there is a danger that group intuition will be confused with 'group think' (see page 91), and a decision will be based on the lowest common denominator. Group intuition is working when it brings together the following three factors:

Needs. Ask the group, 'Do we need to make a decision here? Does the organisation or team or department need to act?'

And as a result of this:

Awareness. The group shares heightened intuitive awareness of the opportunity or the problem through the use of their senses. We can connect collectively when everyone in the group feels deeply and strongly about the outcome.

Belief. We all have beliefs about individual and group capabilities, and, it should be added, nearly always underestimate them. Group intuition draws out belief in what we are capable of as a group or team – both in the room and beyond it.

These three factors are likely to be fashioned by the collective knowledge and experience of the group.

Summary

As intangible as the 'softer' processes may appear, sometimes they are essential to good decision-making. In fact, they are just as important as the 'hard' processes we looked at in Chapter 6. No one should be fearful of these softer processes because the fear can be controlled by putting your idea through the hard tests outlined in the previous chapter. If you have done all you can to gather relevant information in the time you have available to support a decision, you need not be fearful of making the 'jump' when the emotional processes involved in actually taking the decision come into play.

CHAPTER 8

Decisions and actions

Although this book has a linear arrangement, being set out in stages, there is much crossover between the stages. For example, many of the techniques in Chapter 4 (How to Generate Brilliant Ideas) will also be very useful in Chapter 1 for identifying opportunities. The techniques described in Chapter 5 (People Challenges) can and should be used across all the stages.

In this chapter we investigate the critical links between Stage 3, which deals with making decisions, and Stage 4, which discusses putting your decision into action. Much of the content here will be useful in both those stages. It looks at the development of your brilliant idea from three perspectives:

Your own perspective. We use a 'four-box model' to establish how far you can act on your own authority and initiative, and where you have to secure others' approval before moving forward.

The company perspective. Here we look at the size of the idea and how its scale will generate fundamental questions about the challenges the idea will bring.

Looking at your idea from different perspectives can provide valuable insights and give a greater chance of success.

The market perspective. This considers the effectiveness of the idea and links the strategy you choose with your likelihood of success.

The four-box model – where can I act?

The four-box model was originally created by educationist and creativity writer Mark Brown as a way of defining the boundaries of where you can act on your own initiative and where you need to seek managerial (or other) approval. It is a crucial element in both the decision-making stage (3) and the next stage (4), where you put your decision into action. We are using it here because it will do two things for you:

Help you to decide which ideas are self-actionable and therefore have the greatest chance of success because you are able to keep control of every aspect of the idea

Anticipate the levels of involvement and input needed from others during the action stage.

Your decision to act on a particular idea might also depend on which idea you think you have the most control over. The more involvement from others, the less control we are likely to feel.

The four-box model is shown in the diagram below.

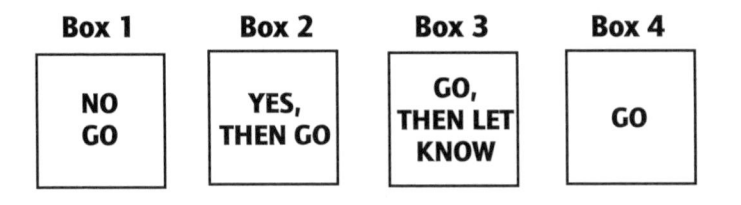

These four boxes illustrate four areas of our work and the freedom we have in those areas to action our ideas. You are free to have as many ideas as you wish in whichever area of the business you want to have them. Actioning them is a separate issue, and we need a framework to help us understand where our freedom exists. This is where the boxes help, and I explain how to use them on the next two pages.

If your ideas are based around the specifics of your own job and how you work, you will need to identify the areas where you have freedom to innovate on your own initiative and where you need to seek managerial approval and inputs early on in the process.

How does the four-box model work?

The four-box model needs two actions. The first action relates to your freedom to innovate within your own job definition.

- Write a list of all the key elements that make up your job. The list is likely to be somewhere between five and 25 things. Try to look beyond the banality of your job description when you do this and look at the true function of what you do and your achievements.

The second action relates to the level of personal empowerment you have of each of these aspects of your job:

- Drop each of these elements into one of the four boxes above using the guidelines below.

NO GO: These are the areas of your job where there is little room for improvisation, new ideas or initiative. For example, in areas where safety or legal compliance might be compromised you need to follow procedures carefully. Even though there may be little room for innovation, we can choose our attitude towards the often mundane stuff that lives here (and develop brilliant ideas for doing it better).

We all have aspects of our jobs that sit in this box. So the key question is: 'Does your brilliant idea compromise anything in the NO GO box?' If it does, the likelihood is that you will have to drop it. If you find that one element of your idea presents a challenge in the NO GO box, you may have to reshape that part of the idea so that any NO GO box violations are removed.

YES, THEN GO: This box captures those elements of your job where approval is needed before you go ahead and do things in a certain way. You can have ideas and innovate more freely than you can in the NO GO box, but first you need to talk them through with others, or with those you report to. You will find that many of your ideas will fit in this box – particularly the bigger ones that impact on other people's work. You will need to collaborate closely with others to ensure your idea's success.

GO, THEN LET KNOW: This is the space in your job where you have the freedom to innovate and apply your ideas in the way you want to. It is useful to feed back to others involved in the process the knowledge of how and what you did and what happened afterwards. GO, THEN LET KNOW encourages initiative and individual growth, and it is the space in your job where it becomes easier to action your ideas. A great example here relates to the company receptionist. Walk into company A and the receptionist seems to be barely alive. Walk into company B and the receptionist has applied his or her ideas and personality to the role. B has applied some GO to the role, but is likely to let someone know that they have done so.

GO: This box represents total freedom. You are in complete control. If your idea is pure GO, then why not GO? Think through the practical issues clearly (by referring to the previous chapters of this book) and then GO for it! This is really only likely to apply immediately to some of the smallest ideas. Bigger ideas will need to progress through the other boxes first.

 Good ideas from Google

An interesting example of how the four-box model can be used in a different way is provided by Google. They allow their staff 20 per cent of their time to 'play' on projects that may or may not be related to their job, but are things that really interest them. This 'playtime' gave them Google Earth (software that shows detailed views of our cities from space) and Gmail (a webmail service that gives users an unlimited inbox). In fact, it is believed that half of the company's new product launches result from ideas generated during this 20 per cent time.

Freedom to think and the time to play with ideas live in boxes 3 and 4. When staff feel that they are on to something good, they will eventually need to tell someone what they are working on if they want to progress their ideas. At that point the ideas become GO, THEN LET KNOW. To actually go ahead with an idea clearly requires a 'Yes', so the idea moves to the YES, THEN GO box.

In this example there is a strong demarcation between the freedom to have ideas (and to have time allocated to experiment) and the decision to go ahead and implement those ideas.

Idea size

Ideas come in different sizes. The biggest ideas will affect the way the business operates at a strategic level. The smallest will concern themselves with the minutiae of your own job. There is great value in having both. There are also many other shapes and sizes of idea that exist between the biggest and the smallest. When deciding which ideas to adopt and action, it is important to understand the implications of applying ideas at those two extremes. The chart opposite will help you to assess some of the criteria involved in taking decisions and the wider implications for the organisations in which those decisions are made.

Does size matter?

The size of an idea may affect both the decision-making process and the subsequent actions required to make the idea go ahead. Some of the smallest ideas can be taken up on your own initiative or with minimal recourse to management. The biggest ideas are tougher to action, but incredibly rewarding when they happen, because of the huge impact they can have if they work. Beware of the fear factor preventing the progression of big ideas. Size is not a reason to give up on your idea – far from it. What it means is that your idea will need to be rigorously thought through at both the decision-making stage (see Chapters 6 and 7) and when you (and your team) devise a strategy to make the idea happen. The success test will be:

> Of course size matters! Some ideas can be put into action independently, but others will need lots of support from others.

How much do you want your idea to happen?

Idea impact – the biggest and smallest

The biggest and smallest ideas happily coexist. Of course, the defining line between the characteristics of the two can be blurred. The chart on below shows some interesting differences between the characteristics of small-scale and large-scale ideas, but these are not absolutes. So, for example, the first point suggests that the smallest ideas produce incremental change, whereas the biggest ideas produce transformational change. There is, of course, no reason why 'small' cannot be 'transformational' or that 'big' cannot be 'incremental'. Or why small ideas can't generate the big wins, and the biggest the quick wins.

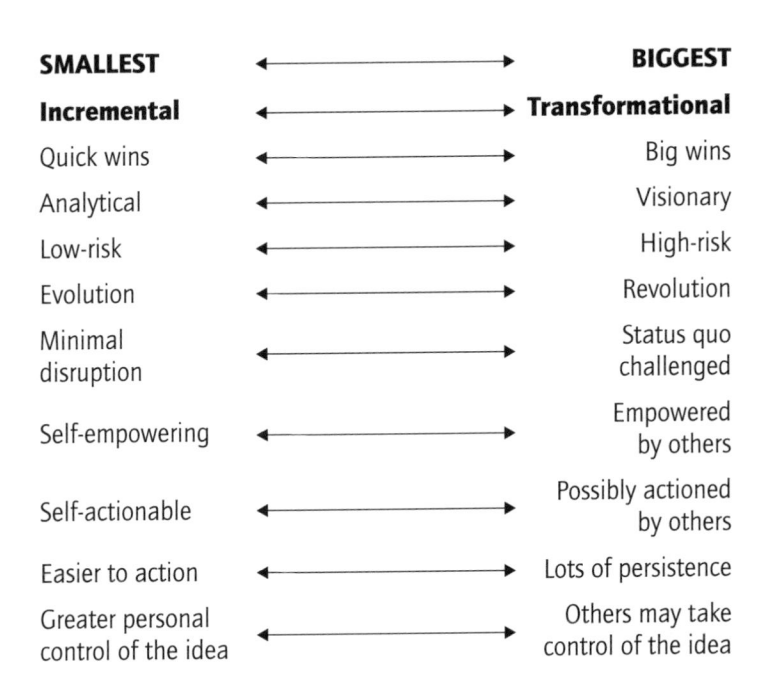

SMALLEST		BIGGEST
Incremental	⟷	Transformational
Quick wins	⟷	Big wins
Analytical	⟷	Visionary
Low-risk	⟷	High-risk
Evolution	⟷	Revolution
Minimal disruption	⟷	Status quo challenged
Self-empowering	⟷	Empowered by others
Self-actionable	⟷	Possibly actioned by others
Easier to action	⟷	Lots of persistence
Greater personal control of the idea	⟷	Others may take control of the idea

Notice that the arrows move in both directions. What the chart says is that at the extremes the smallest ideas will generally show the characteristics identified in the left-hand column while the biggest ideas will usually show the characteristics identified in the right-hand column. Things get more blurred as you move towards the middle, so the characteristics of a medium-sized idea will share aspects of both extremes.

What the chart clearly indicates is that if you want to jump-start acceptance of your idea and you need some quick results, it's best to start small. This is not an argument against launching a large-scale project or challenging the big picture if you feel that that is what's needed, but it is important to recognise the challenges that lie ahead if you take this route. Any challenge can be tough to overcome, but if you want to overcome it enough, you will. Many have succeeded before and you can join them.

A crucial point to remember is that research shows that those who succeed are more likely to be the moderate rather than the high-risk takers. Is there any reason why you cannot start small with your big idea, use market feedback to adapt and change it, and then relaunch on a large scale when you feel the time is right and you have the knowledge and expertise to be more confident of your success? Or to launch the big idea in small, incremental, carefully considered steps?

Have a look at your idea now. Does it show more of the characteristics in the left- or right-hand column? An idea with large-scale characteristics will be more expensive, more challenging and more high-risk than an idea with small-scale characteristics. It doesn't mean you shouldn't proceed with your idea, but it does mean that you should proceed with more savvy and more caution.

Idea effectiveness

During the decision-making process your primary aim will be to establish as far as you possibly can whether the idea is going to work. Many of the techniques described in chapters 6 and 7 will help you to do this. There is a formula that you can apply too.

Idea effectiveness = Strategy × *Chance of success*
(Or 99 = 10 × 10)
The point being that no idea is 100 per cent effective.

There are many factors that will determine the effectiveness of your idea. The formula above suggests two fundamentals that will help you to measure the possibility that your idea will be effective: your strategy and your chances of success. This is particularly so as your ideas get bigger, and especially so if they are the biggest strategic ones.

Once you have formulated your idea, it is time to use the above formula to measure its potential. You can do this by taking the following steps:

1 Apply a value between one and 10 in relation to the quality and depth of your strategy. One is weak, 10 is the strongest. If you have not yet put together a clear strategy, or your strategy hasn't moved beyond 'back of an envelope' thinking, the score here will be low.

2 Apply the same scale to evaluate your likelihood of success. Risk assessment will be a significant factor. High-risk ideas or ideas that are being backed with little research or because little research is available (the paradigm-busting ideas) will have a low score. Small-scale ideas will usually, but not always, score more highly. (Refer back to page 111 to remind yourself of the characteristics of large and small ideas.)

3 Multiply the two scores together and your result equals the likely effectiveness of your idea. In this scoring system 10 multiplied by 10 equals a maximum of 99 – because nothing in life is guaranteed.

How did you score?

Over 80 per cent: Are you dreaming? This score suggests that you might not have been realistic about the likelihood of success and/or the quality of the strategy you have devised to put your idea into action. The biggest ideas will not score this highly because they are likely to be high risk. There will be too many variables to guarantee that your strategy will be close to 100 per cent right at this early stage. If you haven't really considered a launch strategy, or if you want to see if your strategy is strong, you will find it useful to read Chapter 9.

If your idea is a very small one, you should ask yourself the same 'Are you dreaming?' question, but if your assessments are right, a high score indicates that you should go ahead.

Very few ideas will score at this level. Any idea that needs to involve other people will almost certainly be compromised at some point and there will be an impact on anticipated effectiveness as a result.

> The 'idea effectiveness' system can act as a useful catalyst for decision-making, helping to develop a stronger strategy and to look more closely at the characteristics of any project.

50–80 per cent: Very small ideas that involve more than one person are likely to sit here because of the impact of personalities on idea effectiveness. Any ideas with strong, 'big idea' characteristics (see page 111) are unlikely to appear here unless they are closely based on an existing and highly successful idea. Reappraise and be realistic!

30–50 per cent: Many large-scale ideas will appear here. Small-scale ideas with associated characteristics will appear at this level only if the strategy is not yet properly thought through. Read the next section carefully to sharpen your strategy.

Less than 30 per cent: Realistically, the riskiest of ideas – that is to say, those ideas that are the largest and feature most of the large-scale characteristics listed above – will sit at this level. It does not mean that the ideas should not go ahead, but there just isn't the information available to assess the likelihood of success. The strategy at this level needs strong leadership skills, and the idea needs to be directed by someone with a very strong vision and focus.

If you have been entirely honest in your assessment of your brilliant idea, this 'idea effectiveness' system can act as a useful catalyst for decision-making. It covers the necessary ground in both developing a stronger strategy and in looking more closely at the characteristics of both the bigger and smaller projects, as illustrated on page 111.

Key variables in launching an idea

Before we lead into the next chapter, which focuses on strategy, there are four key variables that are often underestimated in the process of putting an idea into action. These were introduced in Chapter 5 as important traits for influencing others. They are looked at here in the context of the likelihood of your idea's success

Reputation

What's your track record? Do you have a good reputation? If you do, others are more likely to back you. Reputation is the primary capital for getting your ideas accepted. If you are 'unknown', it will be tougher to get the backing of others. You will have to work hard to develop other interpersonal skills to compensate, and will need to rely more on the reputation and expertise of others. Your likelihood of success score should be low if you are not sure about your reputation.

Idea support

Whose backing do you have? Remember to talk to your finance department if investment is needed; to your IT department if technical support is needed; and to your managers if people are needed. Who will you talk to? If your intercompany networking has been minimal up to now, and the influence of your idea extends into other people's jobs, you need to increase your level of networking, otherwise your chances of success will be extremely low.

Head and heart

Are you in love with your idea? If you are too enamoured, the depth of your emotions may hijack your ability to reason. Blind acceptance of an idea is like naive infatuation: we say to others 'Isn't he/she beautiful?' and can't understand why they don't share our view. Attachment to your idea is essential and will provide emotional propulsion. However, blind love is irrational. You need to work hard on the rational side of your thinking to ensure that your emotional side doesn't overwhelm you (and everyone else).

> Like love, enthusiasm can blind you to flaws, so work hard to keep your rational side in charge.

Vision

The biggest ideas require a clear vision – a very clear sense of direction and the skill to lead people towards that vision. Have you or anybody else got the high-class leadership skills to achieve this?

This line of questioning is deliberately tough. We often get so wrapped up in the vision of the idea that we forget all the crucial things we need to do to give it life. The assessment stage is where we need the strongest brake. We might not use the brake to its full extent, but we need to slow down. Take a lesson from history. There are so many brilliant ideas that were left on the shelf or did not fulfil their true potential because the brilliant person who had the idea wasn't so brilliant when it came to putting it into practice. Don't waste your chances of success because you didn't go the extra mile to get the strategy right.

Summary

This chapter has provided the essential link between decision and action. Perhaps the key factor that links the two is motivation. When you have made a decision, you and your colleagues must feel 'driven' enough by it to build up the necessary energy in the action place.

In the next chapter we look at different strategies you can develop when putting your idea into action. You can increase your idea's effectiveness by adopting these strategic 'tactics'.

Ideas in the wild

CHAPTER 9

Strategy and launching your brilliant idea

We are now at Stage 4 in the brilliant idea process. After defining the problem-solving or opportunity-taking goal, generating ideas and deciding which ideas are going to help achieve the goal, we now reach the crucial action stage where your idea is launched.

You remain the principal champion for your idea, but by now, at the strategic development stage, you will be working with others who will also champion your idea. If you are now working as part of a team, your idea will be let loose to survive 'in the wild' of other people's ideas and input. Only the smallest-scale idea that impacts just on your own job will not need others' input. You and colleagues now need to devise a strategy for putting your best idea into action. From now on 'you' may mean 'all of you' as well as you alone.

There are several key points to remember at the strategy stage:

- There is no substitute for a positive 'can do' mentality at this crucial stage of action (see Chapter 11).

- Difficulties and challenges have to be recognised and faced, and you will need tenacity to see things through.

- It has been said that a bad idea well actioned may actually do better 'in the wild' than a good idea badly actioned. Your influence, motivation and planning are crucial to your idea's success.

- A clear strategy at the outset provides the best basis for success, but the strategy should not be inflexible. You need to be ready to adapt to change if it will improve the marketability of your idea.

- Be aware of the threat of the 'group think' virus developing at the strategic development stage. This chapter ends with guidance on how to recognise and deal with this common problem.

In this chapter we look at four strategic approaches:

1 **Dealing with drivers and resisters.** All ideas involve driving through change, and change usually generates resistance. How do you identify, react to and resolve the points of possible resistance?

2 **Recognising your intrapreneurial qualities.** Intrapreneurs are employed entrepreneurs, and you are now one of them. What are the qualities required of intrapreneurs at this strategic stage?

3 **Adapting strategy to organisational culture.** What strategies should you use in different types of organisation?

4 **Using guerrilla tactics.** Organisations can be intimidating places. Some take on the characteristics of large armies with powerful forces at work. How do you thrive in this sometimes hostile environment when you might feel that you and your small team are taking on this great force?

You are the principal champion of your idea, but don't forget that you are also working as part of a team.

1. Drivers and resisters

People resist change, and it is likely that your brilliant idea, unless it is so small as to impact only on your own job, will meet resistance. For example, if your idea relates to a bureaucratic process, resistance will vary from verbal opposition to refusal to run the new system. If your idea relates to a new product, you may encounter the 'Yes, buts' in full force. The level of resistance will determine whether or not your idea progresses past the strategic stage. In Chapter 5 we looked at the challenges of working with people, and those lessons apply particularly strongly in this strategic action phase.

To manage any change successfully you need to recognise and anticipate the factors that might lead to resistance to your idea. To do this you need to place yourself in the shoes of the resisters and explore their reasons. What are their personal drivers? Why are they resisting your idea? Next you can work on reducing the impact of those resistance factors. The key things to consider are:

- Be ready to face resistance to the very factors that you believe make your idea brilliant.

- The harder you push the benefits of your idea, the greater will be the resistance to those benefits. (Think back to your responses in childhood: no one likes to be told what is good for them.)

- What to your mind drives the need for change may be perceived as some form of personal loss by the resisters. You think the new system will do great things, but the resisters see only the loss of the old one.

- You can't force people to see benefits. They have to see them from their perspective and believe in them for themselves.

- You can devise a revised strategy based around the concerns of others so that the resistance is minimal or ends.

Opposite is a diagram that illustrates a simple approach to resistance. It is a version of what has been called a force-field diagram in that it illustrates how the drivers and resisters fight each other if the drivers are pushed too hard.

The example used is a continuum of the one in Chapter 2, where we looked at an organisation that has a problem-solving goal based around the reduction of email. They set themselves the goal of wanting to reduce the use of email because their employees had stopped talking to each other. It was decided that a good solution would be to reduce internal emails received to 15 per person per day, and that idea was agreed.

In the left-hand column are the change drivers – in effect, the benefits of the brilliant idea as you see them. These represent the areas in which you are going to promote your idea – 'This is what it will do for us'.

The key to this model is that every time you push too hard in one direction – with the change drivers – you will get an equally strong 'force' coming back to you – from the change resisters. The strategy is based on challenging 'head-on' (but not confrontationally) the likely areas of resistance rather than hammering the drivers home. The driver arrow elongates and the resistance arrow shortens because you recognise, acknowledge and show concern for the key resistance factors. The key is that the 'owners' of the resistance factors can see that you are addressing their concerns.

For example, if the resister is concerned that 'Less management by email' means 'More meetings', how can you counter the argument positively? Perhaps by providing training so that meetings are run efficiently, or by showing management how to brief teams face to face?

Change drivers			**Change resisters**
Reduced volume of email	→	←	My most important tool for communication
We will talk more	→	←	Talking takes up time
Reduction of FYI-type emails	→	←	I am protecting myself
Fewer misunderstood emails	→	←	Less information
Less management by email	→	←	More meetings
Only important emails get sent	→	←	How will I know what is going on?
Time saved	→	←	Loss of ability to respond quickly to requests
Talking is real communication	→	←	Email is easy

2. Recognise your intrapreneurial qualities

A successful intrapreneur needs six key characteristics:

● Leadership qualities

● Persistence (and a thick skin)

● Good management of information

● A 'sharing' disposition

● Ability to balance risk against the likelihood of success

● A democratic approach

Leadership qualities

Intrapreneurs provide leadership, or they identify a leader to move their idea forward. The leader must provide a vision – a clear sense of direction and a defined goal that all those involved in the brilliant idea aspire to.

The leader values the essential contributions of others and is an effective delegator, while recognising the need to maintain overall control. Responsibility, however, cannot be delegated.

Persistence

Success means being persistent without being pig-headed. You need to be tenacious and keep faith with the idea despite the challenges and less-than-helpful reactions. However, don't ignore irrefutable evidence that something about the idea (or the idea itself) isn't working.

Flexibility is key, so be prepared to adapt, reshape or even drop your idea if necessary. Setbacks and frustration need not lead to a drop in motivation. They should be expected. (You need to develop a thick skin too, as not everyone will deliver criticism tactfully.)

Look at how aviation pioneers continually revisited the idea of getting machines to fly and you begin to see how failure and disappointment can be used as spurs to idea improvement rather than reasons to give up.

Good management of information

As we saw in the decision-making phase, control and management of information are essential in idea success, but that mass of information can also be paralysing if you let it control you. Value what is relevant and important; sift out the superfluous.

A 'sharing' disposition

Sharing information is important to an idea's success. Share information with those involved with the idea even if that information brings bad news. Honesty, although perhaps initially difficult, will pay dividends later.

Sharing is also positive in another context. Any successes should be celebrated and shared with those connected to the idea. They will feel appreciated and more attached to you and the idea. Your brilliant idea ceased to be a solo achievement as soon as you launched it into 'the wild'. The success of the idea will build up your reputation, and your growing reputation will make it easier for you to get your next idea adopted.

A warning to the wise: if you flaunt your reputation or claim the success as yours alone, you will lose respect from your peers and your team.

Ability to balance risk against the likelihood of success

In a famous test, psychologist David McClelland once asked young people to throw rings over a peg. An added twist was that the further away they stood from the target, the more points they could score if successful. Some took a high-risk approach, stood a long way from the peg and usually missed altogether. Others were over-cautious, standing close to or on top of the peg, and scored few points. The most successful were those who took moderate risks, calculating carefully how far away they could stand while maintaining a good chance of success.

Modest risk combined with measured strategy provides an excellent success formula for those acting on their brilliant ideas.

A democratic approach

An approach that achieves consensus through open discussion is particularly useful when you do not have a clear sense of which direction to take and you want a spread of views and perspectives. A democratic approach should be combined with clearly agreed decisions and actions at the end of the consultation.

Experience starts to teach us what might happen on the idea's journey, even if it is not a predictor of what will definitely happen.

3. Strategy and organisational culture

Many writers (the philosopher Charles Handy in particular) have studied organisational cultures and identified certain characteristics associated with different culture types. Every organisation has its own distinctive culture and ways of doing things, and your strategy will need to be adapted to the kind of culture you operate within.

In this section we identify four types of organisational culture and the things you may need to consider as you develop your strategy for action.

Power culture

A central power source, sometimes even one person, dominates the power culture. This model is common in smaller, entrepreneurial-type organisations, and in some larger organisations where a person or group of people has been closely identified with past success. However, it is important to emphasise that the central power source may not be personality based. That said, increasingly successful or innovative business people can achieve almost celebrity status within and beyond an organisation (Jack Welch at General Electric and John Browne at BP did this). Even though the dominant person or group may not have day-to-day control of everything, their thinking (business philosophy) will permeate every area of the organisation.

 **brilliant** How to influence within a power culture

- In small organisations the power source is easy to identify, though there is no guarantee that it will be easy to influence.

- It is not a good idea to challenge the authority of the person or persons in power. Emphasising what the core benefits of your idea will do for them will be a key to the acceptance and success of your brilliant idea.

- Organisations with a centralised power base like effective results and may be less concerned with knowing the detail of how you get those results. This scenario does not mean that you should abandon business ethics, but requires clear business focus and positive results: 'This is where it takes us, and this is what we will get out of it'.

- The softer strategic skills of influencing, negotiating and so on play an important part in formulating strategy and gaining approval for your idea. You will need them when dealing with key individuals (such as business advisers or personal assistants) closely associated with the power source.

- Success breeds success. You may gain closer and easier access to the central power source in future because successful individuals get noticed.

Role culture

The role-based culture is often bureaucratic and based on a strong pyramid-type hierarchy, where adherence to rules, job descriptions and satisfactory performance are of central importance. Such a culture is more concerned with the job 'role' than the individual who fills it.

This is possibly the toughest culture in which to activate new ideas because this type of organisation works on the basis that the structure is tight, everything is planned, and too many changes will be disruptive. If everyone performs their role effectively, the organisation functions successfully.

 **brilliant** How to influence within a role culture

- You will need to emphasise the clear, systematic thinking behind your idea if it is to survive. All processes and procedures will need to be thought through meticulously in advance. You will not be taken seriously unless you have done this. (Organisations such as the Civil Service are typical of this cultural style.)

- Working within existing rules and procedures may lead to faster acceptance of your idea than if you try to change them.

- Introduce change gradually. People work in this type of organisation precisely because of the comfort and stability it offers. Change is likely to challenge that comfort and you will need to work hard to soften the sense of insecurity that may result from the implementation of your idea. There can be stability in change, but the change needs to be incremental.

- You may find it easier to launch problem-solving ideas rather than opportunity-taking ones in this culture.

- Expect changes to be incremental. Go for small wins rather than grandiose, high-risk leaps. Hierarchical cultures do not like risk, so minimise it wherever you can.

- It can be dangerous to go above people's heads in the hierarchy.

- The biggest ideas require long-term commitment and a great deal of persistence. Revolution is unlikely to happen in this environment.

- The hierarchical nature of this type of culture means you might 'lose' ownership of your idea as it moves up the hierarchy.

Task-orientated culture

Cultures of this type concern themselves with getting the job done and are usually strongly based around project teams. Individuals with knowledge can expect to be empowered to get on with it, but usually within the team context. Each team has the power to make decisions, and individuals may feel that they have more influence than those within the power or role-based cultures. Teams come with few hierarchies. Seen as the prevailing contemporary model, they struggle when things get tough (particularly when restrictions are placed on money and resources), and revert to the characteristics of power and role cultures to survive.

 **How to influence within a task-orientated culture**

● This is possibly the easiest culture to operate within because there is flexibility of approach and a lack of hierarchy.

● Your reputation will be very important here. What have you achieved in the past? Why should you be taken seriously?

● Take a team-based approach, selecting individuals with the appropriate skills to get the job done.

● Respect is based on your capability and reputation rather than age and experience.

● Keep your team small, dynamic, fast-moving and results-orientated, but don't allow team pride or a natural spirit of competition to develop into an air of arrogance.

● This style of culture breaks down when teams (different project teams, for example) or departments (perhaps sales versus marketing) start to compete with one another for recognition and status. It is important to emphasise that your brilliant idea will be of general benefit. It is not a device to prove that one team (or one person) is better than another.

● Task-orientated culture is the current zeitgeist model to which many organisations and managers aspire.

Personality-driven culture

In cultures where personalities dominate, the organisation is subject to the wants and needs of certain individuals. They may decide to band together in partnership because their needs are better served by doing so; this is a key way in which this culture differs from power cultures. Small consultancy firms and the professions where partnerships are the norm will show these characteristics.

Those who are outside the work partnership will find it difficult to get access to the group and will find it very hard to influence them unless the benefits to the individual personalities are very clear.

These cultures are relatively rare. Those who work in them may have to play a role that is subservient to the dominant individuals. However, those who survive and thrive in the personality-driven environment often do so because they create a very strong personal power base. For example, 'You only get access to the chief through me'.

 **How to influence within a personality-driven culture**

- Many of the tactics you might use in power cultures (see page 132) could work here too.

- Those providing high-level administrative support (powerful PAs, for example) often block access to these personalities. You need to invest time in your relationships with these people.

- Just as the organisation has come together because it sees strength through numbers, so you may find that the same principle works for you.

- Many organisations have pockets of these 'people-type' cultures – groups of individuals recognising that the best way to achieve something may be to club together until their individual needs are satisfied. However, this may not be practical or, indeed, possible, and – regardless of culture – you may need to adopt guerrilla tactics in order to succeed with your idea. In the final section of this chapter we look at different approaches you can use under the banner of the corporate version of guerrilla warfare.

4. Guerrilla tactics

How do the smallest fighting forces manage to take on and often see off a much larger, better-equipped, better-trained force? The answer is that they adopt guerrilla tactics, recognising that if they play to their strengths and don't allow the opposing force to take them on at their weakest point, they might succeed.

It needs to be emphasised that guerrilla tactics against your own organisation are rarely appropriate as an over-arching strategy. Guerrilla tactics should be adopted only in extreme circumstances when all other approaches have failed, or when you see the odds very heavily stacked against you. However, some of the individual tactics are useful adjuncts to other strategies and can be used in most situations.

Why 'fight' in a way that ensures defeat if guerrilla tactics can help you to succeed?

Recognise strengths

The process should begin with an identification of what makes you strong and what makes the organisation strong. Your personal strengths are likely to be based on the following qualities:

- You can respond more quickly to changing circumstances – rather like a small boat being able to change direction more quickly than a tanker.
- You have high levels of motivation.
- You are persistent.
- You have discipline – as a small force, you (and perhaps a few colleagues) can find it easier to control discipline than can an organisation with hundreds of employees.
- You have a permanent role within the organisation.
- You can make small, incremental changes without drawing attention to yourself.
- You are confident that your brilliant idea will yield advantages.

The organisation's strengths may include:

- Control of resources (money, etc.)
- Level and extent of resources
- Power and influence
- Control over employees
- Size (which can be overwhelming for anyone trying to change it)

Guerrilla tactics in action

Despite the term's association with sabotage and destruction, guerrilla tactics are not unethical or destructive in a work context. They are about moving subtly, using your strong points and using controlled persistence to make the organisation, as you see it, better through your idea. Here are some suggestions as to how you might use these tactics:

- You must take the organisation on at the point where you are strong and not where it is strong. Making decisions that cost money and use lots of resources is not a good idea if you don't want draw attention to yourself.

- Keep performing in the key areas of your job – the things you are employed to do. This is the first priority. Your preoccupation with progressing your idea must not detract from your job function.

- Stay disciplined and keep your personal standards high.

- Work to influence individuals first. Don't take on the whole organisation. Start with those who will be least resistant to you. Chip away at their reserve.

Adapt your style to changing circumstances. There is only one (or one team) of you, so you can adapt more quickly than the organisation. Do this by following the Chinese military tactic of *suzhan sujue* (meaning to fight a quick battle to force a rapid resolution):

1 Assess the situation.

2 Identify a moment of opportunity in the situation.

3 Develop a quick action strategy that makes the most of the situation.

This strategy favours fast and small wins rather than the high-risk tactic of going for the big one. You see a person or a department encountering a particular problem for which your idea presents a solution. This might be the time to make your move. In addition:

● Use those conversations at the water-cooler as an opportunity to talk about what you are up to – as a means of spreading subtle propaganda. Individual conversations are crucial to your success in guerrilla warfare.

● Keep your approaches subtle. Sticking your head up and shouting loudly means you become a recognisable target.

● If you really believe in your idea, your persistence will outlast resistance. Make it a battle of wills if necessary.

● Keeping a low profile means never explicitly revealing your vulnerabilities.

Enjoy this tactic! I once interviewed a Mexican political activist and street fighter from the 1960s. (He's now a leading academic.) During the interview he told me that while incarcerated for street fighting with the 'authorities', he learnt 'the value of finding things to enjoy'. Remember, fighting for your idea is part of your life, but, unlike real guerrilla fighters, do not make it your whole life. Maintain your perspective and choose your battles wisely.

Corporate lethargy

There is a kind of virus that lives in many organisations and it spreads quickly among people who spend a lot of their time with each other. This virus is highly contagious and there is a particular strain that spreads an awful affliction – corporate lethargy. Its symptoms include:

- Saying, 'No, we can't do that because...'

- Meetings that generate only one or very few ideas – and ideas that everyone agrees with at that.

- Saying, 'We tried that years ago and we failed. I don't see that you will do any better.'

- Saying, 'So and so won't like it' (thereby delegating the objection).

- Using expressions such as, 'It's a no-brainer' (it is for the person saying these words because they have stopped thinking), and 'singing from the same hymn-sheet' (theirs – and they have only one).

- Inertia – a 'can't be bothered' attitude.

At a more strategic level the signs include closed statements, such as:

'The only way to cut costs is to make staff redundant.'

'The *only way* to grow is through grand acquisition.'

'The *only way* to increase profits is to put the price up.'

The words 'only way' are important here. There is always more than one way to achieve something, and many of the great innovators are those who have disregarded the status quo and taken a fresh look at the situation.

Never are brilliant ideas needed more than when the corporate lethargy virus attacks an organisation; but brilliant ideas alone will not kill the virus. So ingrained is it, and so deeply felt, that all your interpersonal skills, all your great powers of persuasion, all your powers of persistence will be essential currency. You will need to wage war diplomatically. There is no point being a dog that constantly barks – after a while everyone ignores it or you.

Killing the lethargy virus

In order to wipe out a virus, first we need to know what a virus is and what it does.

A virus can lie dormant for many years before becoming active as a result of an unfamiliar trigger.

Our virus sufferers do not regard themselves as a unified force until stirred into action by something unfamiliar that they instinctively want to reject.

A virus can copy itself – but it needs the help of a 'host'.

Our sufferers are very good at cloning themselves throughout your organisation by latching on to the most receptive hosts – those who have a predilection to catch viruses already.

An untamed virus can lead to the death of the host. If the virus catches on and spreads, the organisation dies through inaction.

Now we know what the virus does, we can kill it.

We can protect other cells from viral invasion.

When a virus invades our cells we release proteins called interferons that protect other cells from viral invasion. Because you are strong you can act as a barrier between the invaded and those yet to be invaded. Make them aware of the dangers of their inertia. Make them aware of what your competitors are up to. Make them aware of the consequences for jobs and job security, if appropriate. Make them aware of the positive effects of what you want to do. They might not listen at first, but there is great value in being a stuck record – although not the forever-barking dog. Eventually, someone will listen and discuss the merit in your idea. And then someone else will listen. And then someone else.

Identify the strong and the weak cells.

Our group think sufferers might spend their time and energy spreading apathy and have most success among the already apathetic. Spend your time getting the commitment of the strongest and most energetic people to your ideas. Things will build from there. Identify the fellow 'players': at most, around 10 per cent in any organisation may be all it takes to invigorate the idea through a healthy dose of their energy and attitude. Energy and positive attitude spread far more quickly than apathy because the spreaders of apathy are usually apathetic themselves. Keeping your energy levels up will help to raise the levels of others too.

Viruses can be killed if the host shuts off the invaded area.

This is not really practical for us humans, but some plants have 'learnt' to do this. If all else fails, just ignore the virus sufferers and carry on with what you are doing. In reality, those chronically afflicted may be only 10–15 per cent of the people in your organisation. Many want the cure, even if their innate conservatism makes them resistant at first, and they will be pleased that someone has found a possible cure for them. You are going to be around for longer than the 10–15 per cent because you will always have more energy for the 'struggle' than they will. So mentally wall them off and get on with what you are doing.

Combating the lethargy virus

If the lethargy virus is prevalent in your organisation and is threatening the progression of your idea, you need to think not just about the great idea, but also about adopting a strategy that will chisel away at this syndrome. Part of your strategy might include:

- Using 'soft' guerrilla tactics to outmanoeuvre a huge but undynamic force as described earlier (see page 136).

- Using constructive disagreement as a means of stimulating discussion.

- Taking on the role of devil's advocate at meetings to challenge prevailing views.

- Getting quick wins. Maybe you have an idea that will generate some quick wins and allow you to say, 'Well, in our team we did something new; we did this. And this is what happened.' In other words, offer some evidence that suggests that success is possible. Remember, reputation is what wins you backing from others, and success feeds reputation. But also remember not to wave success in other people's faces and to credit others in those successes.

Above all, do these things in a way that strengthens relationships rather than damages them. Although your main aim is to gain credence for your idea, you are winning allies for the future and don't want to risk alienating them forever.

Summary

In the world of business writing there is perhaps more advice on business strategy than anything else. Undoubtedly, some of the advice is good and usable. But some of it is complex and close to unintelligible, and much of it impractical. The word 'practical' should be an essential part of your thinking. Perhaps the secret is to have a strategy that makes sense, is clearly thought through and, most importantly, can be easily communicated to and understood by others.

CHAPTER 10

Brilliant ideas
and teams

earning to let go of exclusive ownership of your idea is an inevitable aspect of idea development. This first happens when you or somebody else puts together a team to work on the idea. You may not even be on that team. However, the chances are that you will be, and there is an equal chance that you could be leading the team in some way. At this point it is essential that you stop thinking, 'This is my idea'. You are now truly 'sharing' the idea, and the benefits of working in a team will only bear fruit if the other team members begin to share ownership of it.

Letting go can be hard. The sense of ownership you feel for your idea may be very strong. However, you should be pleased at the team involvement because it affirms the organisational commitment and indicates that you are on to something.

Other advantages of working in a team include:

- Sharing the burden. (You cannot do everything on your own.)
- Keeping a range of experts focused on an idea. (This should create a stronger idea.)
- Getting commitment from others. (There is a strategic advantage to involving people early in the process.)

At this point it is also worth noting that successful teams share certain characteristics, as listed below, and you must try to ensure your team has them too.

1 They have a set of ground rules, which they agree to work to.

2 They are results orientated – they get the job done.

3 They set targets and timelines as they work on the idea.

4 Relationships are strong both within the team and between the team and customers and stakeholders.

5 They communicate well.

6 Team members are clear about what they are doing.

In this chapter we cover how you and your team work together in terms of idea generation, brainstorming and roles.

Idea generation within teams

Teams need to generate ideas at all stages of the brilliant idea process, and they can do this in various ways, as discussed in the following pages.

Brainstorming

Since the 1950s brainstorming – concerted group idea generation – has been a chosen method for coming up with ideas within groups. You have probably taken part in brainstorming sessions yourself at various times.

Brainstorming is not a creative panacea. Its limitations include:

- Over-control. Many people would prefer a freer style of idea generation. It can be hard to switch on the creative brain just because someone says, 'Tomorrow at 10 a.m. we will have a brainstorming session'. Others dislike working in a group setting and feel unable to speak.

- Lack of opportunity for 'gestating' ideas. The mind likes to get to work slowly on ideas. Brainstorming does not encourage the slower ways of 'knowing'.

- Unnecessary pressure. Brainstorming creates pressure to produce, which may not be the best environment for free thinking.

- Poor management style. Brainstorming sessions are often badly run, becoming vehicles for the more outspoken members of a group, or allowing premature idea judgement.

But, but, but...

Brainstorming can work wonderfully well if certain ground rules are adopted.

Brainstorming team rules

There are two key pieces of advice you would be wise to heed. First, as the 'owner' of the original idea(s) or as the identifier of the problem or opportunity, you should try not to be the leader or chair of the team meeting as well. Too much power invested in one person runs the risk of team members deferring to that person, and consequently we get a lack of original ideas. In this situation, that's disastrous.

The second piece of advice is not to make brainstorming a 'publicity exercise'. Do you genuinely need help? If not, do not hold a brainstorming session.

Other rules of engagement are as follows:

- All members meet as equals – status is suspended.

- No one idea is more valid than any other, regardless of who has the idea.

- Ego must be suspended. Idea generation is not a competitive sport.

- Piggyback ideas. One idea can spark off a whole train of creative thought on the back of it.

- No toleration of 'Yes, but…' statements. Instead, encourage the 'Yes, and…' approach, which builds on each other's ideas – a version of piggybacking (see previous point).

- No idea evaluation. This is the most common failing in brainstorming because people stop having ideas if the atmosphere becomes prematurely critical. Save the critical judgement for the decision-making stage. Right now we mustn't attach any more worth or value to one idea than to another.

- Be sure that you have people from a variety of organisational disciplines taking part, including those with little connection to the problem or opportunity you have identified.

- Everyone must be a willing participant.

- If you suffer from a lack of ideas, try to imagine you are a completely different group – perhaps a football team or a group of doctors – tackling the same problem or opportunity, or trying to agree a course of action. How might others see the goal? How might they think or react differently?

Remember: having a group working on idea generation in this way encourages buy-in. When others have had input into your idea they feel a sense of ownership of the solution and therefore more committed to it. This 'sharing' approach is essential if you are to get your ideas into action.

Team roles in decisions and actions

When it becomes time to put your brilliant idea into action you need to give real thought to the balance of your team. A range of skills and specialisms will be needed, as will representatives of stakeholder departments. However, big teams are unwieldy and can become ineffective. A team of 6–7 should be the optimum.

Another factor often ignored is the personal qualities that individuals bring to the team. Too often we focus purely on the specialist knowledge that individuals offer. In this section we look at four specific 'roles' that are needed within the team. Most personality profiles focus on categorising people into five or six types (hopeless if, like me, you believe there are 6–7 billion very individual characters out there). The focus here remains strongly on roles, even if the language used to describe them is personal.

Within the team there are likely to be four principal types:

Drivers – the action people

Brakers – the people who challenge the drivers or maybe even stop them

Passengers – the people who have time to think

Maintenance people – those who keep the team tight and bonded.

Drivers

These are the accelerators on the team. They are characterised by a 'can do' mentality – they are the action people.

● They provide an energetic 'face' for the team and can be relied upon to have a go with the idea.

● They are task-orientated and may be less concerned with ways and means of achieving their goal.

● They may well be drivers without a map.

● They may be inflexible and often see only one way (their way) to do things.

Brakers

Brakers provide an essential balance for the drivers and are particularly useful in the decision-making stage.

● They ask lots of important questions, including:

'Have you thought through the practical issues, particularly the allocation of people, time and resources?'

'Have you checked the detail?'

'Have you budgeted properly?'

'Who is going to do what (and when)?'

'How do you know that the idea will not be met with universal apathy when you/we action it?'

● Brakers want facts and information.

● They are often found within departments such as finance, personnel and other administrative areas. But there will be plenty of brakers in other departments too.

● It is easy to be negative about such groups and individuals because they can be seen as people whose *raison d'être* is to limit ideas, creativity and innovation – mostly yours. Even though you might think that way, if you show this attitude to brakers, you will be doomed to fail. Brakers prevent action from being impulsive and badly planned.

● Get brakers on side. A braker in the team makes a great ally. Ignore them and you create a never-ending idea blocker.

Passengers

As they aren't doing the driving, passengers have time to think.

- They are very good at seeing the bigger picture. They are looking out of the window and have time to see what's going on around them.

- They are often the people who come up with great ideas.

- It is essential that passengers are encouraged or given the opportunity to contribute because they are often quiet in a group situation.

- They may be judgemental or cynical, perhaps saying, 'He's a poor driver'. This may be no bad thing as long as negativity doesn't pervade their whole thought process.

Maintenance people

The maintenance team provides emotional glue. Its members keep things going. They repair relationships and bonds. They care about the team.

- They are useful at resolving conflict and disagreements.

- Being multi-sensory, they see where things are going wrong and are able to identify or facilitate the necessary repairs.

- Because they are multi-sensory, they are very good at getting into the customer's world and understanding what the customer wants.

- They are also very good at instinctively knowing when customers and stakeholders are less than happy.

- These are the 'people people'.

About these roles

All these roles are of equal value and should be included in any team.

No individual performs one of these roles exclusively; everyone adopts other roles as necessary, depending on circumstances.

The driver needs to know where the vehicle is actually going, and it is up to you, the leader or others in the team to maintain direction.

These roles assume that great leadership is provided (by you?) that maintains the vision and values of both the team and the idea itself. Vision creates a direction for the team and the idea. Values check the moral 'rightness' of the direction.

 Dynamic innovation at Sony

There can be no substitute for learning from the real world. Let's look at one of the 20th-century success stories that combined great ideas and teamwork.

In post-war Japan an electronics revolution took place that gave birth to what is still the world's second biggest economy. It was assumed that this revolution came about through imitation rather than innovation. Experts know otherwise. Leading business schools have spent many years researching Japanese innovatory practices to see what companies (particularly American ones) can learn from them. Sony is an example of how innovation influenced the development of their new products. Sony believes that:

● A number of different projects running together provides a pool of ideas from which to choose the best. Beware companies or individuals with only one idea.

● The ideas people should work with the customer service people and the people who bring their ideas to the market. This develops a broader perspective and an understanding of how ideas might relate to the outside world.

● Teams should be multi-disciplinary.

● Failure should be accepted as part of the creative process. But don't make the same mistake twice.

● Creative teams should be small so that they can communicate effectively.

● It must be mandatory that each day employees have to come up with one idea to improve the way they do their job, the service they deliver, or product they are developing (or have developed). The Walkman was a great example of this.

And a lesson for those at the top of the organisation:

● Sony senior management created the key targets, but gave freedom to the creative teams to work out goals and solutions themselves.

Summary

Great teams are more than the sum of their individual parts. Bad teams are less than that sum. In all but with the smallest of brilliant ideas you will be working with a team. You should welcome this, not see it as a threat. With a team of good people, you can achieve so much more than you ever could alone. How you work with, manage and lead the team will be key determinants in idea success or failure. Perhaps it pays to remember the old maxim: 'When it is necessary to lead, then lead. When it is necessary to be led, be led.' Learn when to draw back (which might involve emotional detachment from your idea) and when to drive the idea forward.

CHAPTER 11

You and your positive attitude

In work, as in life in general, it is your attitude that determines how much energy and passion you put in and how much you get out of it. It is also your attitude that determines whether your ideas are brilliant and whether they will be put into action.

You cannot switch suddenly into positive mode, or suddenly weave these attributes into your own psyche, simply because a book tells you to do so. Attitude builds over time. Yours may be positive, negative or somewhere in between. If you or your team find your ideas are being turned down, you might need consciously to change your attitude.

This chapter takes a realistic look at the personal qualities required to be successful with your brilliant ideas. We all have those qualities. We just need to bring them to the surface.

Energy and ideas – the 'e' factors

We start this chapter with the 'e' word – energy – and the four 'e' factors that create the energy required to bring your brilliant idea into action.

E is for effort

Most of us come to work prepared to do a job, but we might not be prepared to give absolutely all of ourselves in doing that job. We come through the door on a Monday morning prepared to give a percentage of our 'whole' self. The difference between this percentage (say 80 per cent of our capability) and our maximum ability (100 per cent) is known as 'discretionary effort'. We give some or all of this missing percentage (up to 20 per cent of our effort) at our discretion. The factors that influence our discretionary effort include the way we are managed, the working environment, and the meaning we attach to our job. However, the most important factor affecting our level of effort is personal attitude. This comes directly from you and drives your decision whether or not to apply more of your discretionary effort to ideas and actions. The more you give, the more you will receive. Nothing will change unless you give more. The rewards can be huge if you do.

E is for engagement

The energy supplied by your level of engagement provides propulsion for your brilliant idea. We all know how it feels to be so totally absorbed in creating something we are interested in that we don't notice time passing. We get into a state of 'flow' that transcends everything else. It's a special feeling. No one can force you to become engaged in something if you don't wish to be involved – least of all something that you are not actually interested in. There is little point in channelling your energy into generating ideas for things in which you have little or no interest. It will be very hard for you to summon enough energy to propel them into successful action over time.

Put your effort into what interests you. If you have little or no interest in your job, change your job or change the way you see your job. In order to succeed, you need to put your energy into things you really care about. Your true level of engagement and interest will be put to the test further down the line.

E is for emotion

Your emotional energy is probably the most powerful driver of all. Its impact on your attitude can make or break the success of a project. The involvement of our 'head' is important, but it is with our 'heart' that we feel deeply. Heart will push us furthest when we need to push. When things get tougher, when our idea has been pulled to bits or when it encounters resistance, it is the strength of the emotional connection we feel for the idea that will push us to improve it or to be persistent in our championing of it. You will need your emotional energy because the great feeling you had when you first conceived your idea will be tested to the full when it comes to the implementation stage.

E is for empathy

Your energy alone will not be enough to enable your idea to succeed. You need others' energy as well. All the way down the line – from idea generation through to acting on those ideas – the strength of your relationships at work will be a determining factor in the success or failure of your idea. It is essential to see the world through the eyes of those you are working with. This requires an exploration of their worlds (see page 64). This is about taking a 'we' rather than a 'me' approach. Taking the 'we' approach will get both 'me' and 'we' to where 'me' wants to go.

People can be the greatest energisers or the greatest consumers of your energy. Your attitude and level of empathy will affect whether others' energy joins with yours to increase the power of your idea, or whether they absorb your energy and the idea stalls.

Ideas and anxiety

Anxiety can drain a positive attitude if you let it. Anxiety anticipates an event or chain of events that generates a range of emotions from mild apprehension through to fear. The basis for these emotions could be groundless or very real. Your attitude in dealing with them will dictate whether your idea flies or dies.

You may be anxious about your idea. That anxiety could be based around some or all of the following questions:

● What about the level of risk involved?

● Have I thought of everything?

● What if … happens?

● How committed is everyone else to the idea?

● What about the things I can't control?

Anxiety is often perceived as a negative emotion because of the debilitating effects it can have. However, a degree of anxiety is a good thing because it shows that you care. Care relates to passion. If you didn't care, you wouldn't have the necessary drivers to catapult you into action. These are the steps to follow if you want to use your anxiety positively:

1 Ask yourself clearly what it is that is making you anxious.

2 Use your anxiety to sharpen your thinking about the specific thing that is making you anxious.

3 Use this sharpened, focused thinking to identify what preventative action you can take *now* to reduce the possibility of your envisaged future becoming real.

Anxiety can bring out the best in you because it keeps you one step ahead of possible adverse events.

What is important is that you see your anxiety as a catalysing rather than a paralysing emotion. If you let anxiety paralyse you, it means that you cease to act at your sharpest and stress is the result. One way to help prevent work anxiety from becoming stress is to keep work in perspective. Remember, it is an important part of your life, but it is not your whole life.

Ideas and control

You will have a strong emotional attachment to your idea, and so you should. It is emotional attachment that will propel you in tough times, but this powerful emotion needs to be kept under control. Control in this sense means self-control. Every brain includes a primitive part that was 'wired' back in our evolutionary history to enable us to respond instantly to circumstances where we are under threat: fight or flight – eat or be eaten! We haven't quite lost this intuitive reaction, with the result that when we feel challenged, particularly over something we feel strongly about, we can overact. We let our emotions hijack reason. Your success with your brilliant idea will depend on strong relationships, and although some relationships flourish on impassioned emotional discussion, many do not. Maintaining self-control is essential to the maintenance of good relationships. 'Lose your cool' in the emotional sense and you lose your relationship too. The result? The end of your idea.

Think before you speak:

- Consider the effects of an unconsidered instant reaction.

- Absorb what has been said and try to understand it before giving a reaction.

- Thought-through, non-confrontational questions are a good way to gain that understanding.

- Give a considered rational response to any challenge.

- You do not have to agree, but it is essential to control the manner in which you disagree.

- Don't take things personally.

It is good to have an end to journey towards; but it is the journey that matters in the end.

Ursula Le Guin,
author

Ideas and influence

The extent to which you feel you can act on your ideas will in part depend on the extent to which you feel you have influence within your organisation. It is your ability, as we saw in Chapter 5, to negotiate, persuade and influence others that will be a key success barometer for you. Yet why is it that we all feel we have different levels of influence – even people who are doing similar jobs? Clearly, some have a very different idea about whom they can influence in comparison to others. Your ability to influence is one thing. How far you feel you can influence is another. It is the extent to which you can have influence that is our concern here.

How to create a web of influence

1   Remember, you can have influence over anybody you come into contact with through any communication method.

2   Make a list of people you feel you can influence – and then think again. The first list you make is usually much smaller than the reality. Think about every person you come into contact with. You have influence over everyone you know.

3   Every person you come into contact with includes team-mates, your manager, colleagues in other departments, other managers, personnel and external contacts, including other offices, suppliers, customers at home and abroad, and even those you notice outside the work environment whom you don't even know yet.

4   If you put yourself in the middle of a spider's web and think of the strands of the web as links to all those you come into contact with at work (and elsewhere), you will begin to get an idea of how much influence you really have. The web will be much bigger than you imagined.

5   The web signifies the extent to which you can influence. What matters now is how you use this web.

6   The use of the web to influence does not mean that you become a 'user' of all those who sit on the web. It means that all interactions have mutual benefit. In order to give life to your idea, you need to be ready to make optimum use of your web of influence.

Positive thinking traits

These traits will particularly help you in Stage 4 – the action stage – of the brilliant idea process. They will help you deal with the knocks, challenges and disappointments that are part of the fabric of working life. They will help propel you forward when you need to find a way forward.

Be committed. If you don't truly believe in your idea, or if you are half-hearted in its execution, you won't succeed. Others will take from your lead, and the leader has to set the example.

Be bold. In order to be accepted, brilliant ideas need creative championing. If you champion your idea first, a whole team of champions will follow. Apply your creative mind to brilliant ways of communicating your brilliant idea. Be as bold as you were when you generated the idea itself.

Be responsible. It is easy to point the finger at someone or something else as a reason for your own inaction: 'It's my boss/my employer/the system – that's the reason I cannot act.' However, the real question is always, 'What am I going to do about it?' You might not always be able to say, 'Can do', but you can always say, 'Can try'.

Be resilient. It bears repeating: persistence and resilience are essential for success. The knock-backs, disagreements, cynicism, lethargy and rejection are certainties. The biggest ideas need the most resilient of hearts and minds.

Be flexible. All organisations operate in a spider's web of relationships and influence. They are diverse, ephemeral, frustrating, exciting. Adapt your approach to each person and to each set of circumstances as you find them.

Be self-critical. Not only can you improve your idea, but you should look to improve yourself too. Ask, 'What can I do differently?' and 'Where did I fall short?' Don't beat yourself up if things don't go right, but don't ignore the possibilities for improvement either.

Why do this for my employer – why not do it for myself?

Is your idea big enough to make big money? Or has your big idea been turned down for reasons you don't agree with? If the seed of a desire to 'go it alone' has been planted in your brain, take a good look at where you are before flying the nest. First consider all the positive things that your employed status brings to you and your idea. They give you a great head start.

- Many of us need the security that employed status brings. It can be that very security that helps us have brilliant ideas because we know we have a possible safety-net if things don't quite work out. ('You don't know what you've got till it's gone,' you might say.) Of course, if you need an edge-of-the-seat lifestyle to truly engage with your creative imagination, the entrepreneurial life might be right for you. But not that many of you will survive!

- Being an employee brings you close to the people, resources and infrastructure you might need. You can channel your efforts into the idea rather than into the stuff that might not stimulate you (such as administration or raising finance).

- You have a free consultancy available (in the shape of everyone you work with) who, if you work with them in the right way, can help you to shape, manipulate and massage your idea so that it is the best it can possibly be.

- If you have great self-belief, lots of energy and ideas, and you can lead people (all great traits of entrepreneurs), then you can be a great intrapreneur too. For every entrepreneur, there are many more great people who worked their way up who did much of what they wanted within the context of their job, but were employed while they did it.

Summary

Creative people can be positive people. Indeed, it takes a positive thought process to generate a brilliant idea, so you have already proved that you, like everybody else, have the capacity for positive thinking and attitude. Positive attitude is about being practical, forward-looking and confident. The brilliant idea process will not be easy, and these characteristics will be essential in you if your brilliant idea is to succeed.

We are near the end of the brilliant idea process. But not quite at the end. Being a positive person as well as a creative one, you probably won't want to stop there, and neither should you.

In the next chapter we suggest where you might like to go next. Indeed, the chapter suggests that to stop here might be dangerous both for you and your employer.

The life cycle
of an idea

CHAPTER 12

What happens
to your idea

The majority of ideas do not last forever. They have a shelf life. In this final chapter we look at what happens to ideas over time in the form of an idea curve. It is a simple tool that helps you to look at the life cycle of an idea from conception to death. But, more importantly, it shows at which stage of an idea's cycle it might be a good time to start initiating new ones.

All organisations require their people to have great ideas all the time, even though it might not always seem that way. The majority of the senior managers that I have worked with over the years have identified ideas and initiative as two keys things they want from those they manage.

The idea curve applies to the life cycle of ideas large and small: from the initiation of a new administrative process in your own team or department, for example, to the development of the biggest products or services offered by the largest corporations. Indeed, you can apply it to ideas you have used in your own professional or personal life if you wish. The curve divides into four separate phases, rather like the four seasons of the year, as shown in the diagram below.

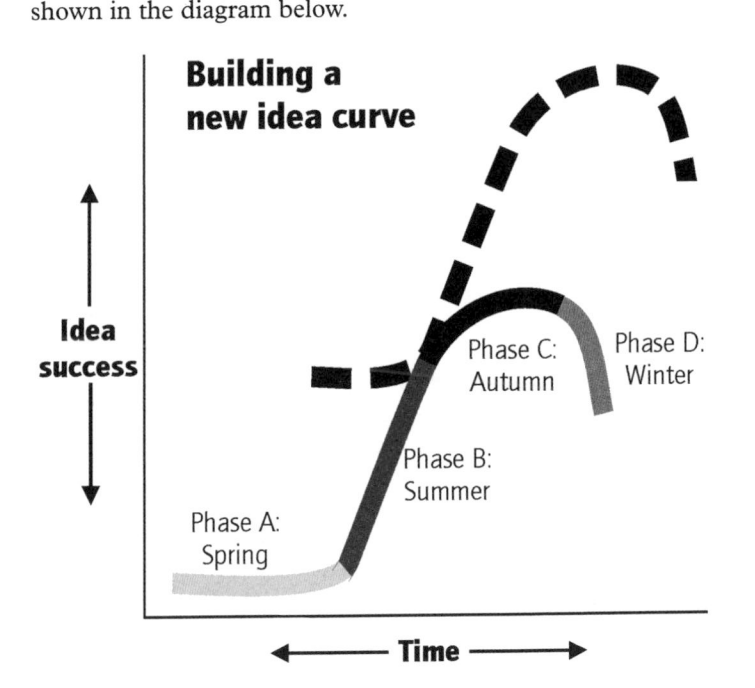

Building a new idea curve

Idea success

Phase A: Spring

Phase B: Summer

Phase C: Autumn

Phase D: Winter

Time

The idea curve shows the danger of thinking that the success your idea (or anybody else's) currently enjoys – and let us assume your idea is a success – will last forever. In Phase A: Spring your idea has just been through the rigour of the 'ideas in the lab' process. Your idea is young and pregnant with potential. Initially, as you get ready for the market, you will be fine-tuning what you offer. If it's a new service or product, you will be listening closely to customers so that you give them what they want. If your idea relates to the internal work of your organisation, you (and your team if you have one) will be working through the practical issues, making sure that everyone that can be thought of has been thought of.

Spring

New life, change, energy, optimism, possibility, excitement, recovery, naivety

There will be a huge number of factors that dictate how quickly that success will come, or if it comes at all, but assuming it does, the idea's success begins to move rapidly upwards into Phase B: Summer. In some cases, the measurement of your idea's success will be easy – new product sales, for example. In other cases, it will be much more difficult, and you will need to rely on subjective methods such as anecdotal evidence to make your judgement.

Summer

Ripening, energy, rapid growth, maturation

The summer phase is the time we really begin to enjoy the fruits of all that labour. But it is also the time of greatest danger. At the moment of our greatest success we are also at the point of our greatest weakness. Why? Because when things are going well we are least inclined to imagine that we need to start thinking about the next curve – a new idea, or ways to make significant improvements to the old one.

In the summer stage of idea creation we often lose the ability to listen. We say, 'My idea is successful; let's ride with that success'. Critically, this complacency can prevent an idea progressing further because we are forgetting to listen to customers and stakeholders.

You might be too busy patting yourself on the back to notice that the need for more of your brilliant ideas is ever-present. That initial energy and initiative can be quickly lost, and the game becomes one of catch-up rather than one of exciting ideas and innovation.

Autumn

Harvest, end of growth, plateau, slow decline

By the time your idea has reached the autumn phase, the idea curve has reached a plateau. We are reaping the benefits – indeed, things may never have been better – but if we have assumed that the good times will last forever, we won't have generated the brilliant ideas needed to launch the next curve.

In the autumn phase you need to let go of your idea. It may be that it is now 'owned' by others who can take it to fruition; it may be that the idea has 'had its day' or a project has come to an end. Becoming too attached to an idea in a fixed form can kill it, so be ready to say goodbye to that wonderful summer phase and prepare for the next one. You need to be geared towards a new seasonal cycle and the next success curve. Winter is an important season for germination and regeneration. It might seem bleak, but there is a lot of activity going on beneath the surface. The joy of winter is that it is always followed by spring – and the start of a new cycle.

Winter

Hibernation, survival, higher chance of death
but also
possibility

Great companies often wither and die. Their once-ubiquitous products or services cease to have a market, or their once-great ideas for generating new customers and clients have been superseded. Maybe they ran out of ideas or they ignored the great ideas they had. Perhaps new products weren't introduced soon enough to replace the old ones, or competitors were more energetic and imaginative with customers and took the market share.

The slowest will start to think about the next ideas in the winter phase of the current idea curve – when the need for them has become obvious. By then it may be too late.

In truth there is no reason why organisations should wither. The best organisations know that the autumn/winter curve of one idea is the spring/summer curve of the next one. The decaying organisation starts engaging in creative thought only when the winter phase warning signs are staring them in the face. The survivors know that winter in one place means summer somewhere else – just as on planet Earth.

Of course, great organisations, large and small, do survive, and they achieve this because they have the flexibility to respond quickly. They quick-think about new ideas at a time when all the evidence suggests that they do not need to – in spring and early summer. In fact, we can go one step further than this. The quick are having brilliant ideas all the time, but it isn't the organisations themselves generating brilliant ideas. Brilliant ideas are generated by people. People like you.

 Xerox – a bad case of complacency

It is often said that if Xerox had run with even 25 per cent of the fantastic ideas it had in the 1970s and early 1980s, it would now be the largest company in the world.

PARC, one of Xerox's research and development facilities, based in Palo Alto, California, had a reputation as a dynamic facility that excelled at developing ideas for the office of the future. It was reputedly the first to develop the laptop computer, pioneered the use of the mouse, and was also in the forefront of laser printing. Hundreds of other technological innovations came out of PARC. So why, in the late 1990s, were Xerox finances in such a parlous state? The word 'bankruptcy' was used more than once.

Business historians may have simplified the story of its decline in the 1990s, but it seems that Xerox was at least partly buying into the following beliefs:

● That the future would be a rerun of the past

● That there would always be a demand for what they offered because of who they were

● That R&D was a 'plaything' – and at that time Xerox had the money to indulge it

● That it had already created the opportunities of the future – but it ignored many of them because it was too blinded by the present

The fact that many competitors have liberally 'borrowed' from Xerox research and created very successful businesses out of it suggests that others (not least Steve Jobs at Apple) could see what Xerox had in its hand when Xerox chose to ignore it. Within the business was the intellectual capital to create a great future. Xerox nearly went under, but has now picked up somewhat, at least in part because it started to pay attention to the value of its own ideas.

Once upon a time, Xerox had been an idea champion itself, taking on inventor Chester Carlson's prototype for the photocopier after it had been rejected by, among others, IBM.

Summary

- Success does not last forever, and the need for brilliant ideas never ends. To this writer at least, having an idea and doing something about it is one of the most personally rewarding things we can do in life.

- Think about the next success while you are growing the current one.

And most of all...

- Having ideas is only the half of a whole. Championing them is the other half. Keep the idea to yourself and the idea remains an interesting curiosity in your own mind, but nothing more than that. Give life to your next idea.

- Ideas without action pass the time. Ideas with action can change the world – your bit of the world or the world itself. How far do you want to go?

Neither in creating nor experiencing may we rest contented with achievement; every day every hour makes new deeds necessary and new experiences possible.

Dr Viktor Frankl,
The Doctor and the Soul

Conclusion

We are all different, and we all express ourselves in different ways at work, but we share one defining characteristic. We are all capable of having brilliant ideas and, indeed, many of us have them all the time. As we said at the beginning of the book, between 80,000 and 100,000 hours (the amount of time you are likely to be at 'work') is a long time to be bored, uninterested and disengaged.

Maybe you have read this book because you were unclear about how to put your ideas into action? There can be immense satisfaction in doing something that made a difference; where you conceived an idea at the start and saw it through to the finish. Where you got a group of committed people together as a team and made something happen that was positive.

So why not start engaging with the creative side of yourself? And then follow up those brilliant ideas with a large dose of action. A good time to begin is now. I hope this book has got you started on that very fulfilling road.

Bibliography

Adams, James: *Conceptual Blockbusting* **(Basic Books, 2001)**

A great book on overcoming all those barriers we have in the creative thinking process, many of which are self-imposed. Despite its slightly off-putting title, this is a very readable and stimulating book.

Borg, James: *Persuasion* **(Pearson, 2005)**

Contains his seven crucial communication skills for persuading others. There is perhaps nothing original in identifying those skills (and there doesn't need to be), but he writes about them with great originality.

Brown, Mark: *The Dinosaur Strain* **(ICE Books, 1993)**

One of the best books on why organisations wither and die, and what you and your organisation can do about it.

Gerber, Michael: *E Myth Mastery* **(Collins, 2005)**

This book was written for entrepreneurs. It has much that is useful for ideas that create new parts of a business or take the business off in a new direction. Great for small organisations.

Handy, Charles: *Understanding Organisations* **(Penguin, 1999)**

The best 'how it all works' business book ever written.

Miller, Douglas: *Make Your Own Good Fortune* (BBC Active, 2006)

Describes how to create and act on opportunities in all walks of life.

Miller, Douglas: *Positive Thinking, Positive Action* (BBC Active, 2005)

I hope it does exactly what the title says.

Pinchot, Gifford & Pellman, Ron: *Intrapreneuring in Action* (Berrett-Koehler, 1999)

The long-awaited sequel to *Intrapreneuring* (1985) and a defining book for the person or team who wants to get ideas into action in organisations.

Rickards, Tudor: *Creativity and Problem Solving at Work* (Gower, 1988)

An older book and, as the title implies, particularly strong on problem-solving.

Von Oech, Roger: *A Whack on the Side of the Head* (HarperCollins, 1990)

Clever, fun and a brilliant tool for opening up your creative imagination.

The Innovation Climate Questionnaire

Organisations who wish to test their climate for innovation can find more information at:

www.innovationclimatequestionnaire.com

The questionnaire tests your climate around 13 dimensions known through rigorous research to be key predictors of the suitability of your organisation's climate for innovation, idea generation and creativity. The questionnaire has been developed over the last 15 years, and is based in part on original pioneering work by Goran Ekvall.

Acknowledgements

Mark Brown, educationist, creativity writer and former Visiting Professor of Innovation at Henley Management College, for the four-box model, which was developed through his own research. Also thanks to Mark for allowing me to dip into his 'library' of thoughts and ideas.

Professor Charles Handy – the piece on cultures (Chapter 9) was inspired by his book *Understanding Organizations* and the Greek god metaphor he uses (originally found in his book *The Gods of Management*).

Stuart Moran, Berkeley alumnus and member of United Nations Volunteers, who gave me 'The play' story (page 50) and showed me the video of it on YouTube in a Macedonian hotel foyer.

Adam Gee ('Arkangel') who leads Channel 4's 'The Ideas Factory', and from whose blog I took the Jonathan Ive quotes. They originally appeared in *Ten 4* magazine. Also for other inspirational thoughts and the opportunity to air early versions of some this material on his various blogs.

Madlib, J. Dilla, Brian Eno, Ashkenazy, the Flamingos and Sigur Ros for the music while I was writing this book.

Piscine Laghetto, purveyors of fine swimming pools that allowed me to keep my 'cool' while writing.

Sarah Sutton, Trish Burgess and Emma Shackleton, who between them must take most of the credit for making this book readable and publishable. The errors are mine.

Nigel Roberts – mobile phone shaker borrowed with thanks!

About the author

Douglas Miller is a successful writer and trainer throughout Europe, specialising in positive attitude, creative thinking and leadership. This is his fifth book. He can be contacted at: doug@dougmiller.demon.co.uk